In Tribute to Adam Petty   **THE PETTY FAMILY ALBUM**

2

The Petty Family Album

IN TRIBUTE TO ADAM PETTY

Pattie and Kyle Petty with Dustin Long
Photography Editor: Tom Copeland

NORTH WILKESBORO, NC, 1975: KYLE AND RICHARD IN VICTORY LANE

First published in the United
States of America in 2002

by UNIVERSE PUBLISHING
A Division of
Rizzoli International
Publications, Inc.
300 Park Avenue South
New York, NY 10010

Adam Petty, Kyle Petty,
Richard Petty, and Lee Petty
names and/or likenesses
used under license by Petty
Marketing Company, LLC.
Sprint and the diamond logo
are trademarks of Sprint
Communications Company
L.P. Paint and decal design
copyright © 1999 Sprint.

© 2002 Petty Enterprises, LLC

Printed in the United States
of America

Library of Congress Catalog
Control Number: 2002103947

Cover and book design:
Brad Simon and John Klotnia,
Opto Design

For their particular generosity
the publisher would like to
extend a special thank you to
Don Hunter, for more than 45
years of amazing NASCAR
photography, Kevin Kane, Bill
Livingston, and the ISC
Archives.

SPANNING GENERATIONS **TOP** LEE PETTY DRIVING HIS 42 CAR IN 1949 **BOTTOM** NEARLY
FIFTY YEARS LATER, ADAM PETTY DRIVING A LEGENDS CAR, A SMALLER VERSION OF
WHAT WAS DRIVEN IN THE EARLY DAYS

HIS EFFORT would not have been possible without the help of many people. Thanks go to the Petty family: Kyle, Pattie, Austin, Montgomery Lee, Richard, Lynda, and Maurice for taking the time to share their memories and stories. Thanks also go to those consulted for this project.

Many others were especially helpful with this book: Martha Jane Bonkemeyer, Tom Copeland, Barbara Davis, Bonnie Davis, Doris Gammons, Jim Hannigan, Kathie Parson, Stacey Sauls, Robn Sorrells, Bob Zeller, Charles Miers, and Jane Ginsberg.

Thanks also to my editors at Landmark Newspapers for allowing me to do this project: Bill Bern, Tom White, and Eddie Wooten. Special thanks go to Scott Blanchard, Mary Fox, Gary Long, Bob Pockrass, Jim Slater, Sherry Slater, and Rea White, who have inspired me and taught me valuable lessons through the years.

And I'm indebted to the countless others who helped me improve as a journalist and as a person. Last, but not least, I thank my brother, Derek, my mother, Sylvia, and my father, Tom, for all they have done.

Dustin Long, January 2002

I WOULD like to thank Kyle and Pattie for letting me visually document many of their family moments over the past four years. The time that Adam gave me, along with help from Stephen Patseavouras, will never be forgotten. Many of the images in this book would have never been seen if not for the hard work of many photojournalists and researchers throughout the history of racing. Special thanks go to Dustin Long, T. Taylor Warren, Buz McKim, Kathie Parson, Martha Jane Bonkemeyer, David Chobat, Dorsey Patrick, Don Hunter, Ritchie Petty, Kevin Kane, Bill Livingston, and Rebecca Cremonese. I am grateful to my mentors Randy Davey, Bob Jordan, and fellow photographers at the News & Record who have molded me into the photographer I am today. Without them, I would have never been successful.

The biggest thanks go to my wife, Llewellyn, my children, Graham and Callie, my parents, Tom and Judy, and my brother Bryant. They are the ones who have to put up with the many missed family outings to make things like this book possible. Thank you.

Tom Copeland, February 2002

KYLE HAD THE PERFECT AUDIENCE IN ADAM

FOREWORD

NO WORDS OR PHOTOS CAN BRING BACK ADAM. But tucked in the pictures of him and his mementos are memories of our oldest son that will never leave us. We fondly recall his energy, enthusiasm, and dedication toward racing. We also remember how he matured into a man, yet remained a little boy inside. Those memories inspire us to raise money for the Victory Junction Gang, a camp where children with life-threatening illnesses will be able to go and not worry about their ailment. The camp, which is being built in Adam's honor, will be a place for those children to play, laugh, and share big smiles, as Adam was known to often flash.

Adam encouraged us to move forward with Victory Junction Gang before his accident. It is one of the reasons why we dug through family photos for this book and shared stories that might not be familiar to all fans of the Petty family. We wanted to celebrate Adam's life with the fans and provide them with a keepsake, while also doing something for the camp. Proceeds from this book will go to the camp, which is scheduled to open in 2004.

Life is never easy. It has been hard for us since Adam's accident. Words cannot describe the pain and anguish of losing a child. That's why each day we spend with each other and Austin and Montgomery Lee is so important and why we want to build this camp. So that these children, who often spend much of their time in hospital rooms, will have a place to be children again. And mothers and fathers can see their children smile.

KYLE AND PATTIE

SOMETIMES WHEN I LOOK BACK on the beginnings of Petty Enterprises, when my daddy used to work on the car in the old reaper shed behind the house, I wonder, "How could a group from Level Cross, North Carolina, accomplish so much in stock-car racing?" You just have to thank the good Lord. Some people are just destined to do certain things, and some are destined not to do certain things, you know what I mean? Why did Daddy meet Mother? Why did Daddy start racing at age thirty-five? Why did my brother, Maurice, and I follow? Why did Kyle? Why did Adam? Why did Adam die in a crash? I can't pinpoint the reasons why, so I just say it's life. I don't know why I won 200 NASCAR races and seven championships. I'm no different than anybody. I'm no smarter. But I went along with it and tried to be nice to everybody through the years since I was given such a special life. While there are many mysteries we can't understand, we just have to look at each day as another opportunity to appreciate life and make things a little better for others. Although Adam's death has not been easy for the family, his spirit guides us to complete the Victory Junction Gang camp for children with chronic and life-threatening illnesses and their families. Once finished, the camp will help make the lives of those children and their families a little better. Adam would be proud.

RICHARD PETTY

FROM THE BEGINNING, Sprint's sponsorship of the Number 45 car has been a pleasure, due in no small part to Adam Petty and his family. Adam's winning attitude and attention to his fans as well as to Sprint as his sponsor were in line with the way Sprint strives to treat its customers. Adam had a wonderful demeanor and character and was truly a fine young man. Few of us in the Sprint family will forget Adam, or the way he represented our company and furthered the Petty family tradition.

Bill Esrey

BILL ESREY
CHAIRMAN AND CEO OF SPRINT

ALMOST SEEING DOUBLE. BROTHERS AUSTIN AND ADAM PETTY, DAYTONA, 2000

LEVEL CROSS

T he roads are no longer dusty, the farms not as big. Yet Level Cross, North Carolina, exudes a rustic charm. The rural community is a place where the song of birds transforms into a symphony when joined by the rustling of leaves, clip-clopping of horses and … rumbling of engines.

This is the home of the Pettys, NASCAR's first family of stock-car racers. It is here that a family dynasty began in 1949 when Lee decided to start racing at age thirty-five. Sons Richard and Maurice followed their daddy into the sport. Their children followed. And on down to Kyle's nineteen-year-old son, Adam, the first-ever fourth-generation pro athlete to compete at a sport's highest level and heir to the family-run team until his fatal crash on May 12, 2000, at a racetrack.

Although distraught by the tragic event, the family continued to race. Kyle put on his driver's uniform three weeks later for the first time since the accident. That day, he climbed into a car that once had been driven by Adam, sat in Adam's seat, and drove a car that had Adam's name above the driver's side door. Why do it? Because there was a race, and that's what Pettys do.

"It's all we know," Kyle says of racing.

It's all they've done in Level Cross, a place so small it does not have its own post office, where the family's progress is evident at the race shop. It all started when Lee turned the reaper shed next to the house into his race shop and the A-frame from that building remains more than fifty years later.

While many NASCAR teams built concrete castles to house their cars, the Pettys added to their facility only when they needed, creating a collection of asymmetrical white buildings of various heights and lengths. Although many NASCAR teams are based an hour's drive south of the Pettys, in the area of Charlotte, North Carolina, the family refused to move.

"This is where we grew up," says Richard, renowned for his record 200 career NASCAR victories, seven championships, and an artistic autograph served with a smile. "This is where we established our families. I've been real fortunate that racing has given me the opportunity to go to Australia, go to Europe, go to Canada, go to wherever, and I've never been anywhere where I didn't like something about the place. But I've never been anywhere I've liked as many things as I like here—the weather, the people, the terrain."

Home is never far when Richard is at work. The two-story Depression-era house where Richard and Maurice were born sits across the driveway from the race shop. Maurice has lived with his family in a house on the other side of Branson Mill Road from the race shop and his child-

PREVIOUS SPREAD RICHARD AND LEE, OUTSIDE THEIR GARAGE, NEXT TO A PLYMOUTH, IN 1962 TOP (LEFT TO RIGHT) EARLY RANDLEMAN, NC; ELIZABETH PETTY'S HOME IN LEVEL CROSS, TODAY

hood home since 1964. Richard and his wife, Lynda, live about three miles from the race shop. Three of Richard and Lynda's four children live within about twenty minutes of them.

To those in Level Cross and Randleman, a town of about 3,500 residents four miles down the road, the Pettys are just neighbors and friends, not famous racers.

"I think that by staying here among our family and among our friends, that no matter how successful Richard became or how famous he became, he never lost touch with his roots," Lynda says.

Richard served sixteen years as a county commissioner. Lynda served sixteen years on the county school board. They and their family have donated money, time, and racing memorabilia to aid local groups, from Level Cross's volunteer fire department (station 43, in honor of the number Richard made famous) to Randleman High School to local youth sports teams.

"If they had been the kind of family that wasn't willing to give back to their roots, [Richard] would have made a name in racing, but he wouldn't have made a name and [Lynda], too, in their giving and their generosity," says Martha Jane Bonkemeyer, a lifetime Randleman resident who went to high school with Lynda and started working at Petty Enterprises in 1967.

Randleman celebrates the Pettys each year with a downtown festival called NASCAR Day, which stretches down Main Street and past the miniature statue of Richard near the town's main intersection. In 2001, Richard and Kyle signed autographs as they do nearly each year, and were joined by Kyle's son, Austin. The festival also includes amusement rides, arts and crafts, and a fireworks show sponsored by Richard and Lynda.

The community found another way to honor the Pettys with the Richard Petty Randolph County Golf Classic. Held every year since 1992, the event had raised about $250,000 by 2001 for the North Carolina Jaycees Burn Center. David Caughron, executive director of the Randleman Chamber of Commerce says that for 2002 and beyond, proceeds will go to the sixty-two-acre camp the Pettys are building for children with life-threatening ailments.

"We just felt like we needed to give back to the Petty family," Caughron says.

THE PETTY FAMILY HOME IN LEVEL CROSS THAT LEE BUILT TO REPLACE THE HOUSE THAT BURNED DOWN WHEN RICHARD WAS SIX-YEARS-OLD

BORN FROM A SMALL REAPER SHED IN 1954, PETTY ENTERPRISES TODAY IS A 14-BUILDING COMPLEX

Adam could be ornery as a youth. Just like any kid, he also enjoyed having fun, especially when he went to the Petty Enterprises complex.

The women who work in the Richard Petty Museum laugh as they recall him charging into the tin-roof building, which displays family trophies, race cars, and souvenirs. He often headed straight for the cash register, punching in a sale of $1 million and asking if that would distort their bookkeeping. Others recall the child's voice boom on the shop's intercom system with bogus announcements or him playing somebody's voice mail message for all to hear.

Anne Fogleman, who handles Richard's fan mail among her duties, remembers those times. But Adam remains with her in more than memories.

"He gave me the name of Momma Anne," says Fogleman, who baby-sat Adam when he was a toddler and later discussed life and religion with him when the teenager stopped by her desk to grab some bubble gum. "People call me that to this day.

"Even as an adult when he was nineteen years old, he still called me Momma Anne. When he had his first team come in to meet me, he introduced me as Momma Anne. They said, 'Momma Anne?' And he said, 'Yeah. My Momma Anne.' "

KYLE AND PATTIE'S FIRST HOME IS A SHORT DRIVE FROM PETTY ENTERPRISES

A VIEW OF THE PETTY BARN, ADAUMONT, NAMED BY TAKING THE FIRST TWO LETTERS OF BOTH ADAM AND AUSTIN AND THE FIRST PART OF MONTGOMERY LEE (GUMMY)

NASCAR

Winston

ARAWAY

TURN

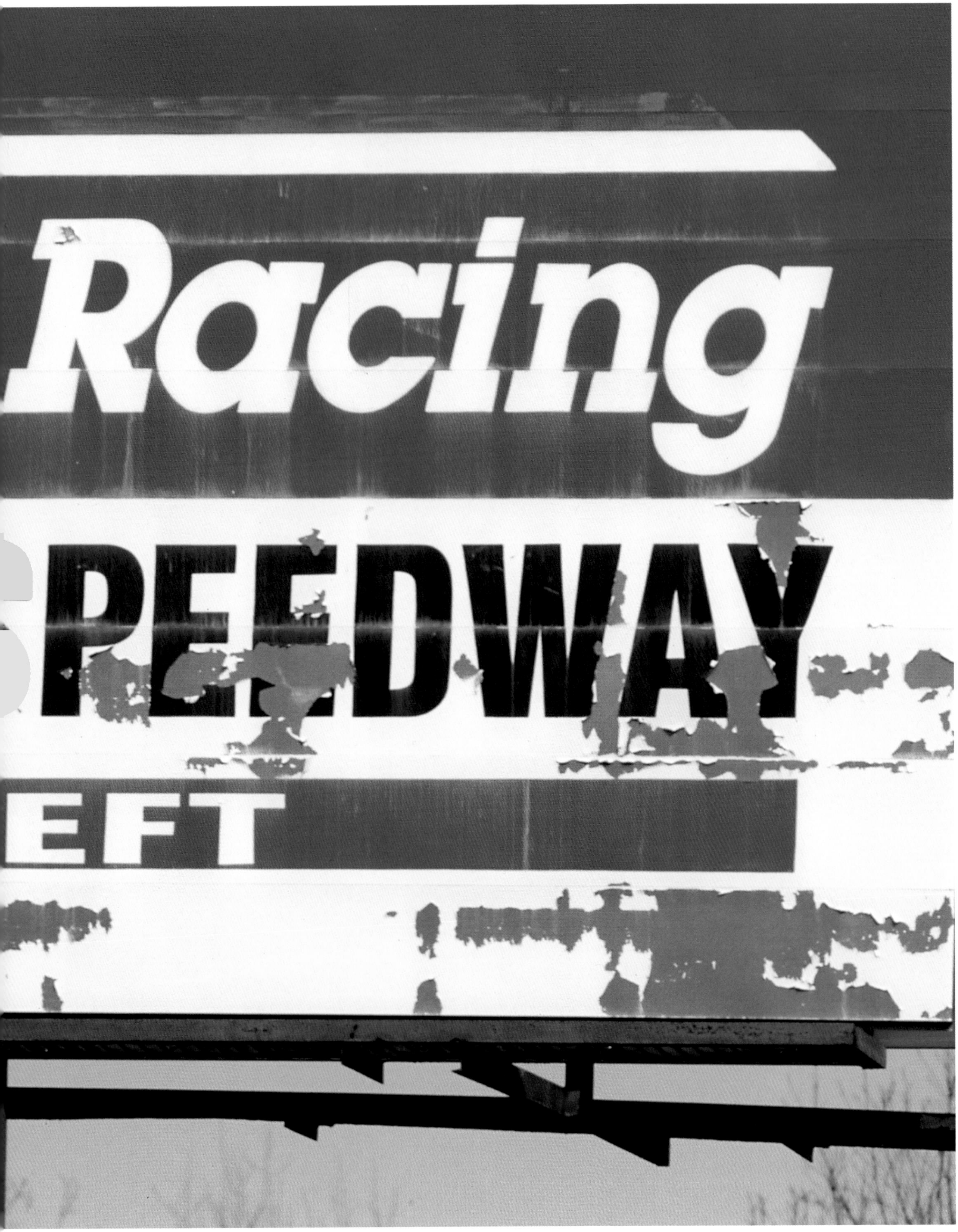
Racing
PEEDWAY
EFT

THIS AND PREVIOUS SPREAD JUST A FEW MILES DOWN THE ROAD FROM THE PETTY SHOPS IN SOPHIA, NC, IS CARAWAY SPEEDWAY, WHERE ADAM GOT HIS START

LEVEL CROSS

It was a place where Adam was just a kid, not a race driver or a famous name. He and Stephen Patseavouras often went with other friends to Badin Lake, about a forty-minute drive from Adam's home, to ride Jet Skis and play on inner tubes as a boat pulled them.

"We'd get down there and goof off all day," Patseavouras says of the man-made lake, which has 115 miles of shoreline and a maximum depth of 190 feet. "A little R and R. We usually had three tubes together, and we towed them."

The boat often swung from side to side, so the inner tubes would bump into each other. Patseavouras says that Adam, the lightest of the group, often went flying off his inner tube. That just made the day more fun.

The day after Adam won his first ASA race in 1998, he and Patseavouras celebrated by playing at the lake.

"He enjoyed being at the lake," Patseavouras says.

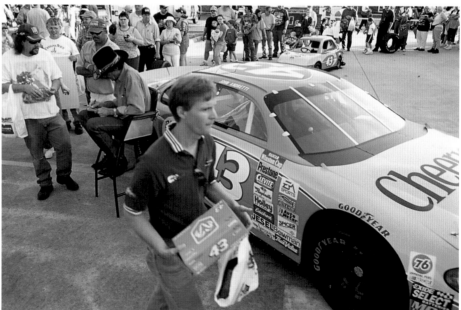

RANDLEMAN CELEBRATES THE PETTYS EVERY YEAR WITH NASCAR DAY, A FESTIVAL FILLED WITH AUTOGRAPH SIGNINGS, AMUSEMENT RIDES, AND FIREWORKS.

RICHARD PETTY

On behalf of the Randleman Chamber of Commerce, the City of Randleman and the people of our community, we dedicate the scaled down replica of Richard Petty in honor of over 35 years of dedication to NASCAR racing and our community. Richard is not only our hometown hero, but our friend and neighbor.

Family Life

FAMILY LIFE

Growing up during the Depression, Lee learned the value of money. So when he decided to make his living in racing instead of his trucking business, he had to make other changes. Often he sacrificed speed for smarts on the track. Lee didn't worry about having the fastest car because one didn't receive any extra money for speed. Instead, Lee made his car more durable and took care of it during the race so that he could finish and earn more money. While he won a lot, Lee also was consistent, finishing in the top ten more than seventy-five percent of the time in his 428-race career. That success allowed him to make enough money to support his family and his racing, beginning a family heritage that spans four generations. His best season was 1959, when he won his third championship and earned $43,590, the only time in his driving career he made more than $27,000 in a season. Racing proved a wise investment for Lee, who entered the sport after watching local races with his brother Julie in the 1940s. They figured they could do as well and did. They built a 1937 Plymouth with a Chrysler in-line engine, and Lee won in his first race in 1948.

Maurice says Lee's success was no surprise, recalling his father's victories in late-night races with moonshiners on back country roads. Lee thrived on competition. It's how he met his wife, Elizabeth. They first met after Lee played a baseball game one day, and it wasn't long before they were married.

Lee, who died April 5, 2000, at age eighty-six, also taught his sons discipline, building a base for his family's future. He kept his sons busy, whether it was going to a junkyard to fetch car parts, helping with the race car as soon as they got home from school, or picking up rocks on the unpaved road near the house and placing them on the family's gravel driveway. Even after retiring from the sport in 1964, Lee often went to the race shop next to his home to make sure the team was working hard. "He wasn't happy when we didn't do good," says Dale Inman, who served as crew chief for all seven of Richard's championships.

"He didn't like that at all. He didn't hold back about telling you that either. He wanted people to work."

Lee's wife, Elizabeth, a proper Southern woman in dress and etiquette, taught her boys a more gentle side. She was against alcoholic products sponsoring the family's race cars. As car manufacturers withdrew their support by the early 1970s, teams were forced to find other ways to fund their racing. They looked to companies to sponsor their cars. Thirty years later, Petty Enterprises remains the only NASCAR Winston Cup team that does not permit alcoholic beverages to advertise on its race cars.

"She was very adamant that we would not have alcoholic beverages on our cars," says Lynda, Richard's wife.

PREVIOUS SPREAD FAMILY REUNION AT THE BEACH IN CHARLESTON, SC
TOP (LEFT TO RIGHT) MAURICE, LEE AND RICHARD; SNOWBALL FIGHT: MAURICE AND RICHARD

"We don't go around condemning people that work for beverage companies. We just have our convictions about things and that happened to be one of them. There again the Lord has blessed us to give us a sponsor like STP for twenty-nine years and now with General Mills, and we've never had to go to an alcoholic beverage."

Another of the family's convictions is its faith and service toward others. Church projects, community projects, or helping out a neighbor are just a few of the many examples of the family's generosity.

"The whole family just said, 'Golly, look at how lucky we are to be able to go and do and have the conveniences that some of the other people that we grew up with don't have,' " Richard says. "So you say, 'OK this is a thank-you back to the good Lord,' I guess—'Hey, thank you, man.' "

The family also remains humble despite its success. Instead of just saying "hi," Richard often greets people with a "Hey, buddy" while he flashes that famous Petty smile passed down to Kyle and Adam. While they all are comfortable in formal settings, they are just as at ease in jeans and a denim shirt. That matches their personality. They are as easy to talk to as with any friend, and as forgiving.

An example is how Kyle treated Ernie Irvan in the early 1990s. A crash triggered by Irvan in 1991 at Talladega collected Kyle, leaving him with a broken leg and forcing him to miss several races that season. Irvan never visited Kyle in the hospital. Irvan never spoke to Kyle about the accident until Kyle approached him one day at the track. The next year, Irvan was hospitalized after a crash. Despite car owner Felix Sabates' objections about visiting Irvan since he had not visited Kyle after his crash, Kyle and Sabates went to see Irvan in the hospital.

Sabates recalls another episode that shows the humility Kyle learned from his family. During their nine years together as car owner and driver, Sabates and Kyle never had a contract, just a handshake agreement. After the 1993 season when Kyle finished fifth in the points, Sabates handed his driver a sheet of yellow legal-pad paper. He had written what he would pay Kyle for the upcoming season on the paper. Kyle tucked it in a pocket and headed for a sponsor appearance after the pair arrived in Las Vegas. At one o'clock in the morning, Kyle called Sabates and told him to come to his room immediately. When Sabates arrived, Kyle asked his boss about what he planned to pay him.

"Kyle, man, that's all that I can pay you," Sabates remembers telling him. "He goes, 'You're paying me too much. I'm not worth that much.' He said, 'How about you cut my salary back and put the money into the race team?'

"Can you imagine a race car driver coming to a car owner, saying you're paying me too much money? That tells you about the guy."

And about his upbringing.

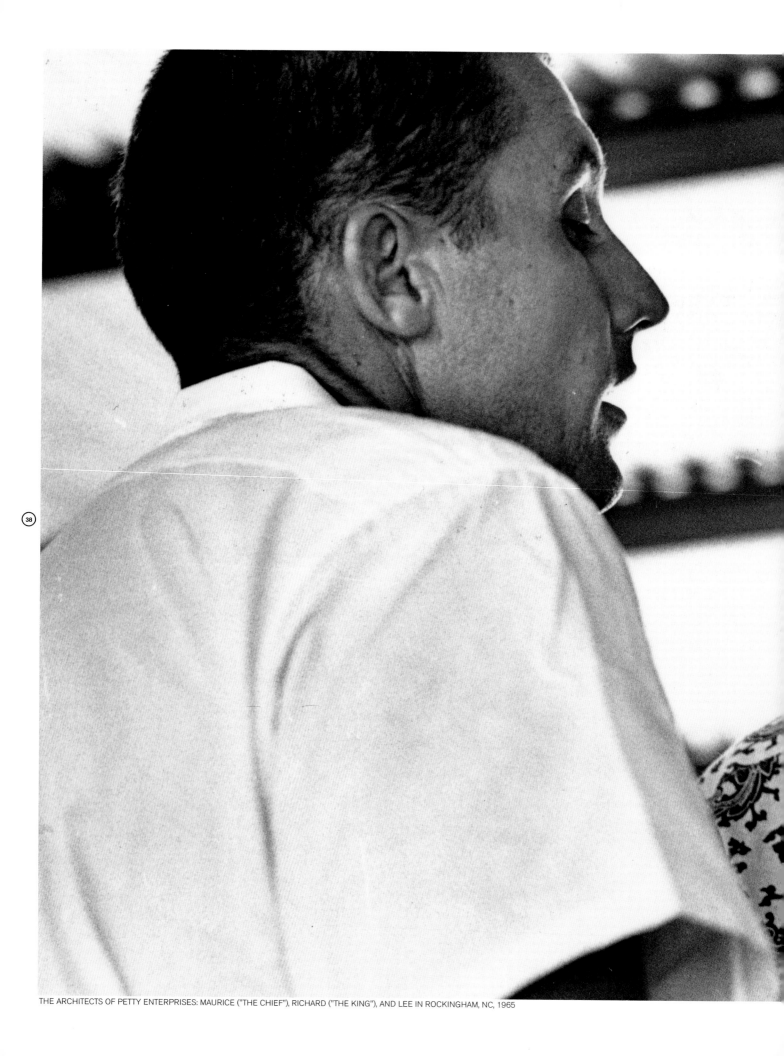

THE ARCHITECTS OF PETTY ENTERPRISES: MAURICE ("THE CHIEF"), RICHARD ("THE KING"), AND LEE IN ROCKINGHAM, NC, 1965

LEE PETTY ON A ROAD TRIP, 1956

LEFT TO RIGHT RICHARD, KENNETH "RED" MYLER, RALPH EARNHARDT, AND LEE PETTY, 1957

RICHARD AT THE "CARWASH", 1950s

COUSIN DALE INMAN AND RICHARD AT HILLSBOROUGH SPEEDWAY, NC, 1950s

FAMILY AND FRIENDS: DALE INMAN, RICHARD, AND MAURICE AT THE TRACK, 1978

WORK'S CUT OUT FOR THEM: RICHARD AND LEE, 1950s

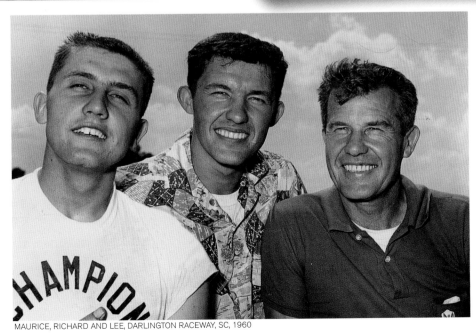

MAURICE, RICHARD AND LEE, DARLINGTON RACEWAY, SC, 1960

JIMMY MARTIN, DALE, AND MAURICE ON PIT ROAD, 1977

44 A DAY NOT AT THE RACES: **LEFT TO RIGHT** LISA (WITH BABYSITTER), SHARON, A FAMILY FRIEND, AND KYLE IN ST. AUGUSTINE, FL, '60S

RICHARD AND SHARON, 1965: THE YEAR THE PETTYS GO DRAG RACING (THEY WERE AMONG THE CHRYSLER DRIVERS TO BOYCOTT HALF OF THE SEASON AFTER NASCAR BANS CHRYSLER'S HEMI ENGINE)

RANDLEMAN, NC, '60s: EASTER SUNDAY AT THE OWENS FAMILY HOME
FRONT ROW LYNDA, LISA AND RICHARD **BACK ROW** SHARON AND KYLE

TOP BACK AT THE RACES: RICHARD'S FAMILY AND FRIENDS ARE HIS MOST ARDENT SUPPORTERS, DAYTONA, 1966 **BOTTOM** RICHARD'S DAYTONA WIN, 1973

FINAL DAYS OF RACING: A FAMILY FAREWELL FROM RICHARD AND LYNDA, WITH ANNOUNCER BARNEY HALL, IN ATLANTA, NOVEMBER 1992

Even if they didn't have the same last name, the members of Adam's team were like family. It's one of the reasons why he insisted they all eat dinner together at a restaurant near the track each night. Often, they went to an Outback Steakhouse if there was one anywhere nearby. That way Adam could eat his grilled chicken and broccoli.

"His big thing was every single night at the race track he wanted all of us to go out together," says Chris Hussey, Adam's crew chief.

"Every single night we did. No matter how bad a mood you were in, how bad the day at the racetrack had been, how long you had worked the night before and you wanted to go to bed at eight o'clock, it was 'Nope, we're going out to eat.' "

Adam shared other times with his team. Shortly after he bought a burgundy Corvette in 1999, he drove it to his race shop and allowed any of the crew guys to drive it. A few did.

"That's just how he was," says Stephen Mitchell, a member of Adam's crew. "Nothing he had was too good for anybody else."

ROCKINGHAM, 1992: AUSTIN AND ADAM TRAILING "THE KING" **TOP** BARRY DODSON, PATTIE, AND KYLE AT THE TRACK IN THE LATE '70S

ADAM, GUMMY (ABOVE), KYLE, AND AUSTIN: ONE OF THE CHILDREN'S FAVORITE MEMORIES WAS KYLE WINNING AT CHARLOTTE, NC, IN MAY 1987, BECAUSE HE BOUGHT THE FAMILY A POOL WITH PART OF HIS WINNINGS

ALTHOUGH RACING KEPT KYLE ON THE ROAD, THE FAMILY TRIED TO DO AS MUCH TOGETHER AS POSSIBLE: AT KYLE'S SISTER LISA'S WEDDING, 1987

GETTING READY TO RIDE THEIR HORSES

Austin's last Christmas Day with Adam was special. It wasn't the holidays that made the 1999 day meaningful. It was mopping his big brother's race shop, which housed Adam's Busch Grand National cars.

"He prided himself on that building," says Austin, who is nineteen months younger than Adam. "This was his race shop. His cars were in there. You walk in there—'Hey, that's my office. I don't go in there, but that's my office. See that car over there, that's my race car. That's my name on top of it.' He prided himself on all that stuff.

"I remember it was Christmas Day and you do the whole Christmas scene, get up at six o'clock in the morning. By eleven o'clock, you're dead tired again.

"So I had laid down on the couch and about twelve o'clock, he came in. 'You want to go mop the floor with me over at my race shop?' The place had just been cleaned Friday. This was Saturday. We went over and mopped the race shop. It was cool because, one, he had asked me to do it, and, two, it was getting to spend time with him, because he was gone so much."

GETTING READY TO RIDE IN THEIR FIRST PLANE

PATTIE AND KYLE MET AT THE RACETRACK. THEIR FRIENDSHIP GREW WHILE TAKING BIBLE STUDY CLASSES TOGETHER, AND THEY SOON FELL IN LOVE. KYLE PROPOSED TO PATTIE BY BUYING HER A HORSE AND PUTTING THE DIAMOND IN THE FEED BIN.

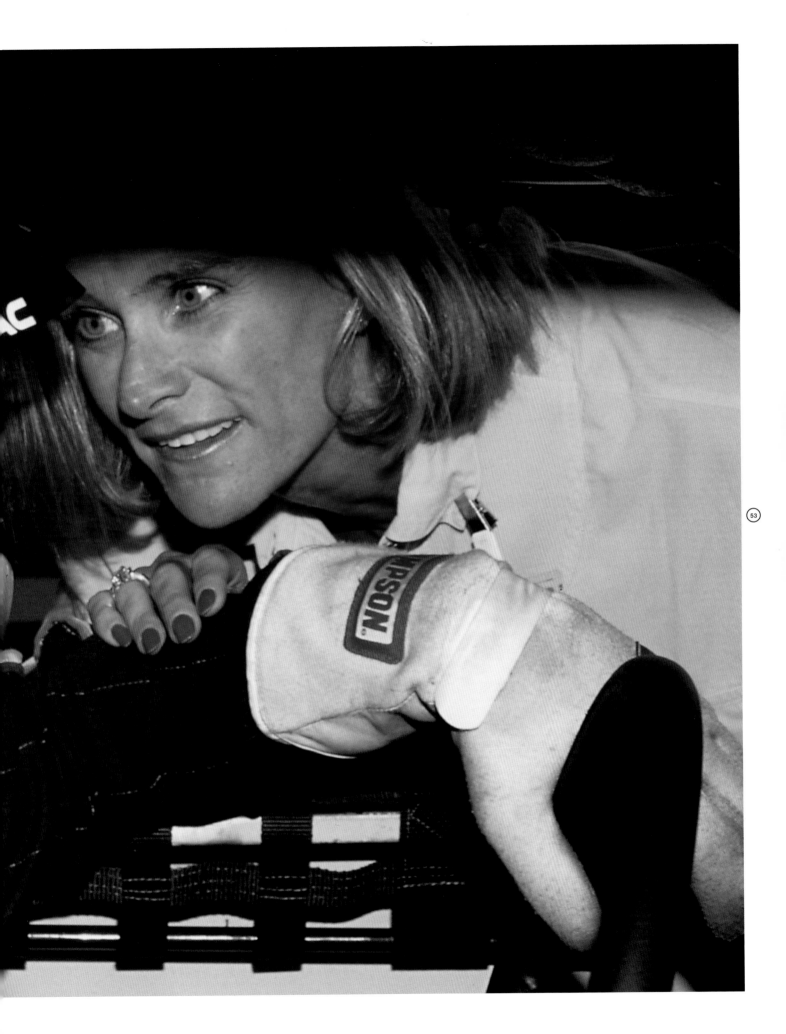

Legacy

Yes, they did the same thing, but each of the Petty men who raced had unique personalities and styles, from Lee's blunt approach to Kyle's flamboyance. Even so, a thread connected past with present, father with son, great-grandfather with great-grandson. Desire.

"The more effort you put into it, the better you ran," says Maurice, Richard's younger brother, repeating a mantra the family has followed for more than fifty years.

It started with Lee. He did most of the work on his car when he entered NASCAR's first event in 1949 at Charlotte Speedway. While Lee rolled the car that race, crinkling the roof and ripping off the hood, he exited the mangled mess undaunted and uninjured, except for a cut. His only problem was that he had driven the wrecked car to the track, a common practice in the sport's early days, and had to find a way home. He did and kept on racing.

"He dedicated himself and said, 'OK, if I work on that car, then I can make a good living for my family,' " Richard says of how his father approached racing. "And so his whole concept of racing was to make a living out of it. It wasn't any glory. He didn't like any part of that. It was strictly a monetary deal, the way he could express himself and make a living for the family. That's just the way he looked at it."

Lee's work ethic could be seen in his thick arms, strengthened by driving a car without power steering. The series' first three-time champion won fifty-four career NASCAR races with the first one coming on October 2, 1949, at Heidelberg Speedway, a half-mile dirt track near Pittsburgh.

Among his most memorable victories was the 1959 Daytona 500, the first race on the 2.5 mile Daytona International Speedway. Lee, Johnny Beauchamp, and Joe Weatherly, who was not on the lead lap, crossed the finish line three-abreast, making it difficult to declare a winner. NASCAR officials sent Beauchamp to victory lane. Three days later, NASCAR awarded Lee the victory after photographic evidence showed Lee's white Number 42 car crossing the finish line a couple of feet in front of Beauchamp's car.

Seeing that success gave Richard, who helped work on the car, the itch to race other than on the roads near his family's Level Cross home. One day, Richard asked his dad if he could race at the track. "Come back when you're twenty-one and we'll talk about it," Lee told him.

When Richard turned twenty-one in 1958, there was little to talk about.

"I come in and I say, 'I'm twenty-one,' and he said, 'There's a car,' " Richard says.

"There was no argument about that. He made up his mind that that's the way it was going to be. He knew I was coming back."

PREVIOUS SPREAD A BORN NATURAL: ADAM MUGGING FOR THE CAMERA AT 7 MONTHS AFTER GRANDPA RICHARD WINS THE DAYTONA 500, 1981
TOP (LEFT TO RIGHT) PETTYS AND THEIR CARS: LEE, RICHARD, KYLE AND ADAM

Sixteen days later, Richard made his debut in NASCAR's top division, finishing seventeenth in a nineteen-car field, in Toronto. He crashed after being bumped by his father, who was chasing the leader as they lapped Richard's car. Better days were ahead, though. The first of Richard's record 200 victories came on February 28, 1960, at Charlotte Fairgrounds. Richard went on to win the Daytona 500 seven times—a mark that is unequaled—and seven championships, tied only by the late Dale Earnhardt. No year was better for Richard than 1967, when he won twenty-seven of forty-eight races, including ten in a row.

"We never thought anything about it," Richard says of the streak.

"Our job was to do the very best we could, and that was to win races. It was one of those deals where you went through and you win a race and you come home and you didn't think about what you done last week, you were thinking about, 'Hey, we've got a race next week, we've got to go win it.' If you went and won it, you came back and said, 'OK, what's next?' "

More victories. Richard's final win came on July 4, 1984, at Daytona, when he nipped Cale Yarborough in a race attended by then-President Reagan. That car later was sent to the Smithsonian Institution and placed in the National Museum of American History.

Even with the victories, it was how Richard treated the fans that made him

"The King." Richard was known to stay hours after a race until every fan received that looping autograph he first perfected in a handwriting course at Kings Business College in Greensboro, North Carolina. His signature remains as distinct as his silhouette, with the long neck, sunglasses, and cowboy hat. Fans continue to seek the autograph of NASCAR's winningest driver. Whenever he stops in the garage area, a crowd of people slowly encircles him, seeking that signature or a photograph or just to the chance to tell friends back home, "Hey, I saw Richard Petty up close. And, man, is he tall and skinny." Of course, Richard remains thin, in part, because he had more than half his stomach removed in the late 1970s because of ulcers. Even that hasn't slowed Richard.

Kyle continued the family's tradition in racing and expanded upon his father's fan-friendly demeanor. Kyle first competed in an ARCA race in 1979 at Daytona, a week after marrying Pattie, and won. He made his Winston Cup debut that August at Talladega Superspeedway, finishing ninth.

While Kyle has not won as much as his father or grandfather, he had his success on and off the track, which included a brief country-music career early in his racing career and a performance at the Grand Ole Opry. He's won eight races with his first one occurring on February 23, 1986, at Richmond International Raceway. That victory made him the first third-generation driver to win a Winston Cup race. While

some might have questioned his dedication early in his career, few doubt his hunger to return Petty Enterprises to the glory it once knew.

Either way, it matters little to Kyle. He once said that he'd rather be remembered for helping sick children than for a racing career. While many will remember him for both, his greatest legacy could be how he has helped others, whether through his charity motorcycle ride across the country or by making hospital visits or by helping local charity efforts.

Adam shared those qualities. Once a chubby teenager who gulped soft drinks like water and ate greasy foods as if they were a basic food group, he worked to slim down and become a better driver.

His determination was evident when he began working out with his father, a friend, and Mark Mauldin, who was hired as strength and conditioning coach late in 1996.

"I saw something in him then that I knew would make him successful in what he was doing," Mauldin says, "because sometimes I would try to make it hard, to see if he would give up, and he never gave up. I knew he was a pretty special kid when I saw him do that."

It came naturally. He was, after all, a Petty.

CLOCKWISE FROM TOP LEFT BEFORE THEY RACED, THE PETTY MEN LEARNED TO WORK ON THEIR CARS: LEE; KYLE; ADAM; RICHARD

DAYTONA BEACH COURSE, 1954: WITH 54 VICTORIES LEE WAS NASCAR'S WINNINGEST DRIVER, UNTIL RICHARD SURPASSED HIM

LIFE'S DEFINITELY A BEACH FOR LEE AS HE ENJOYS HIS DAYTONA SUCCESS

OFFICIAL CERTIFICATE OF SPEED

Annual Speed Tests - Daytona Beach, Florida

THIS IS TO CERTIFY THAT LEE PETTY

DROVE A 1954 Chrysler Coupe

THROUGH THE MEASURED MILE FOR A ONE-WAY SPEED OF 123.41 MILES PER

HOUR AS RECORDED AND CHECKED BY NASCAR OFFICIALS.

THIS IS AN OFFICIAL DAYTONA BEACH SPEED RECORD.

DATE February 18th 1954 SIGNED Bill France

NATIONAL ASSOCIATION FOR STOCK CAR AUTO RACING, INC.

Official NASCAR
Modified Stock Car Racing
Rules and Regulations
for 1949

NASCAR HEADQUARTERS:
800 MAIN STREET, SELDEN BUILDING
DAYTONA BEACH, FLORIDA

NATIONAL ASSOCIATION for STOCK CAR AUTO RACING
NATIONAL HEADQUARTERS, 800 MAIN ST., DAYTONA BEACH, FLORIDA

★ RACE DRIVER - OWNER ★

Issued to MR. LEE PETTY

Address ROUTE 1, RANDLEMAN

City GREENSBORO State N. C.

Age Date of Registry 6-17-49 No. 0-53

Nearest Relative

City

Issued by Bill France

1 9 4 9
•

The undersigned hereby acknowledges that he is familiar with the rules and regulations of the National Association for Stock Car Auto Racing as authorized by the Board of Governors at the annual convention, and agrees to abide by them in all competitive events sanctioned by NASCAR. The undersigned also agrees to do everything in his power to further the sport of stock car racing.

Signature

CLOCKWISE FROM TOP LEFT OFFICIAL RACING DOCUMENTATION: SPEED CERTIFICATE; 1949 RULE BOOK; ORIGINAL NASCAR DRIVER'S LICENSE SIGNED BY NASCAR FOUNDER BILL FRANCE

MAURICE, LEE, AND RICHARD CELEBRATING THE SUCCESSES OF 1964

BELOW LEE'S TROPHY FROM THE 1959 INAUGURAL DAYTONA 500

DAYTONA, 1977: PROUD LEE WITH RICHARD

DAYTONA, 1974: KYLE, SISTER SHARON, AND LYNDA WITH RICHARD IN VICTORY LANE

NORTH WILKESBORO, NC, 1977: RICHARD RECEIVES A ROSE FROM PATTIE, AS A MISS WINSTON GIRL, WHO MET KYLE ON THE FIRST DAY ON THE JOB

DAYTONA, FEBRUARY '79: NEWLYWED KYLE WINS HIS FIRST ARCA RACE, WITH ELIZABETH, LEE, PATTIE, AND RICHARD

CHARLOTTE, SEPTEMBER '98: RICHARD, KYLE, AND ADAM CELEBRATE ADAM'S FIRST ARCA VICTORY

ABOVE RIGHT ODESSA, MO., JUNE 2, '98: ADAM'S ASA VICTORY

DAYTONA BEACH COURSE, 1954: LEE RACING

JUN • 55

67

WEST MEMPHIS, AR, 1950s: LEE CRASHES INTO A GUARDRAIL AND (WITH CAR) LANDS IN THE WATER. LEE AND RICHARD WORK ON THE CAR ALL NIGHT FOR THE NEXT DAY'S RACE; DUE TO RAIN RACE IS CANCELED

LEE AT DAYTONA BEACH, 1954

LEE AT DAYTONA BEACH, 1948 **BOTTOM** LEE AT DAYTONA BEACH, 1957

THREE DAYS AFTER NASCAR UNOFFICIALLY DECLARED JOHNNY BEAUCHAMP THE WINNER OF THE INAUGURAL DAYTONA 500 IN 1959, THIS PHOTO VERIFIED THAT LEE PETTY (MIDDLE) DID INDEED BEAT BEAUCHAMP (NUMBER 73) TO THE FINISH LINE. THE TOP CAR BELONGED TO JOE WEATHERLY, WHO WAS NOT ON THE LEAD LAP

THE DAYTONA BEACH COURSE BEFORE NASCAR MOVED ITS RACES TO DAYTONA INTERNATIONAL SPEEDWAY IN 1959

70

ASHEVILLE-WEAVERVILLE, NC, 1956: LEE TAKES THE CHECKERED FLAG. RICHARD RAISES HIS ARM IN SALUTE

LEE RACING JIM PASCHAL, WHO WON NINE TIMES FOR PETTY ENTERPRISES
MIDDLE WINSTON-SALEM, NC.: LEE RACING AT BOWMAN GRAY STADIUM

MARTINSVILLE, VA, 1953: DRIVERS MEETING BEFORE THE RACE, MANY IN THE STANDARD UNIFORM OF WHITE T-SHIRT AND PANTS

LEE IN THE 42 CAR AT DAYTONA BEACH, 1957

RICHARD RACING AT HILLSBOROUGH, '60s

ASHEVILLE-WEAVERVILLE, 1967: RICHARD'S STREAK OF TWENTY-SEVEN RACE WINS (TEN STRAIGHT) EARNS HIM THE MEDIA TITLE "THE KING"

No matter how many times it happened, Chris Hussey admits he would be a bit nervous when he got a late-night message from Adam.

"I would be on my way to work and check my voice mail on my phone and have a call from Adam," says Hussey, Adam's crew chief. "It was always,

'Oh, no, what's he done,' because you'd look at the time stamp on it and it would 11:45 the night before.

"It would be him leaving a message: 'I'm over here at the shop sweeping the floor. Just wanted to call you and tell you I appreciate everything you do for me.'"

DAYTONA,1972: RICHARD LEADING THE PACK

BRISTOL, TN, 1967: RICHARD BLEW A MOTOR JUST BEFORE THE FINAL LAP, WHILE LEADING. HE OFTEN SUCKED ON A WET TOWEL TO KEEP HIS MOUTH MOIST

DAYTONA, JULY 4, 1984: PRESIDENT REAGAN LANDS JUST IN TIME TO WITNESS RICHARD'S 200TH AND FINAL NASCAR VICTORY

DAYTONA, JULY 4, 1984: RICHARD EDGES CALE YARBOROUGH FOR THE VICTORY

BELOW DAYTONA, JULY 4, 1984: VICTORY LANE CELEBRATION

DAYTONA, 1974: RICHARD SNOOZING AFTER A LONG DAY

KYLE RACING FOR MELLO YELLO, EARLY 1990S

Chris Bradley was always with Adam. Bradley was Adam's friend and crew chief in the ASA series in 1998 until he was killed in a pit road accident during a race at the Minnesota State Fairgrounds. Adam wore *CCB*, Bradley's initials, on his racing uniform after that.

The incident happened when Bradley decided to make an adjust-ment under Petty's car without telling any of the crew. When the jack man dropped Adam's car, the signal for the driver to leave, Adam ran over Bradley, not knowing his crew chief was underneath.

"He had a pretty strong faith in God, and I think he prayed a lot about it and thought a lot about it," Kyle says of how Adam dealt with the death. "I think he got to a point in his mind where there was nothing he could have done different.

"It wasn't something that he ever talked to me a lot about or he ever talked to Pattie a lot about. Sometimes he would make comments about it—that he wished Chris were there to see him run good."

DOVER, DE, 1995: VICTORY

KYLE LEADING THE WAY

CHARLOTTE, NC, 1987: KYLE AND TEAM

DAYTONA 500, 1993: KYLE LEADING THE FIELD FROM THE POLE AT THE START OF THE RACE, WITH DALE JARRETT BESIDE HIM. KYLE LATER IS INVOLVED IN AN ACCIDENT WITH BOBBY HILLIN. WHEN HILLIN APPROACHES KYLE AFTER THE ACCIDENT TO EXPLAIN WHAT HAPPENED, KYLE FLIPS HILLIN'S VISOR DOWN, RESULTING IN A FINE FROM NASCAR

(89)

WHILE THE SPORT HAS CHANGED THROUGH THE YEARS, SOME THINGS HAVEN'T. CARS WILL ALWAYS NEED PIT STOPS
OPPOSITE PAGE LEE, IN 1948 **TOP, LEFT, AND BOTTOM RIGHT** KYLE **MIDDLE RIGHT** RICHARD

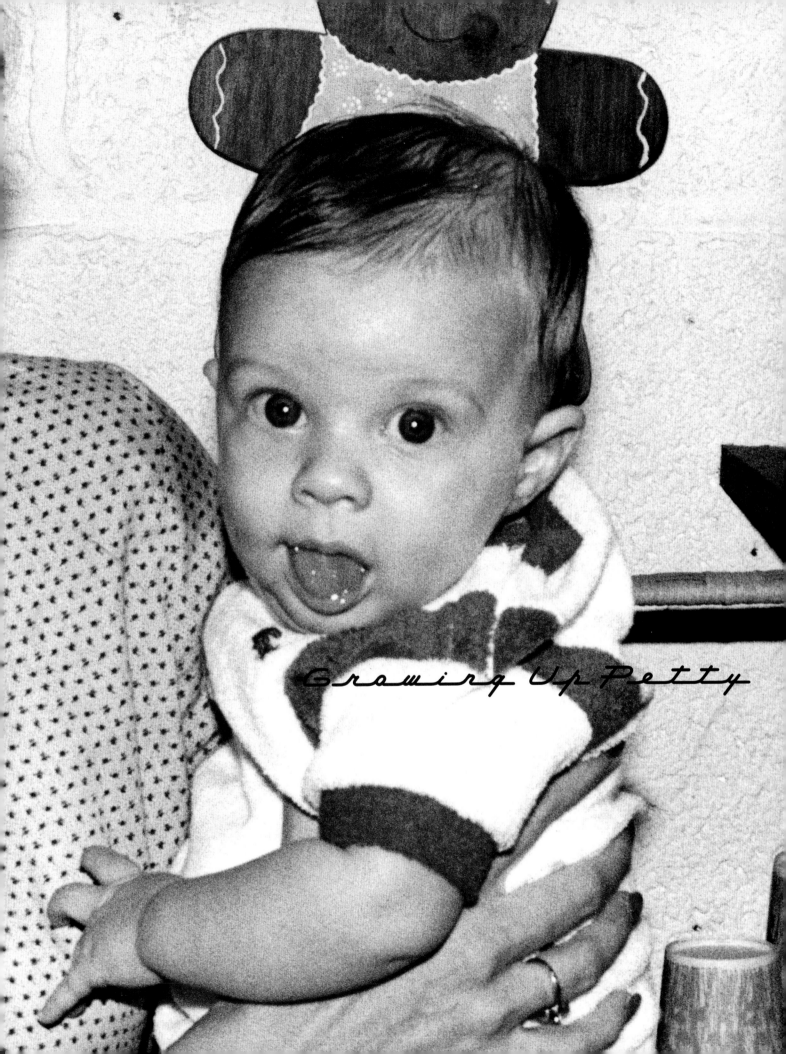

Growing Up Petty

GROWING UP PETTY

Adam didn't seem to mind the commotion. Dressed in red overalls, a red-and-white checkered shirt, red jacket, and a red-and-blue sock cap, the seven-month-old sucked on his pacifier as his grandfather Richard lifted him in victory lane after winning the 1981 Daytona 500.

Even then, Adam's future seemed set. Many people expected him to race, to follow a path blazed by three generations. Friends sent racing-themed clothes, blankets, and knickknacks to Kyle and Pattie after Adam Kyler Petty's birth on July 10, 1980, in High Point, North Carolina. The first grandson of Richard and wife Lynda was a big event. Literally. Adam measured twenty-four inches and weighed about nine pounds at birth.

While others might have looked at Adam as destined to race and carry on the family tradition, the Pettys didn't. Adam showed early signs that he would race. When he was a year old, Adam was walking, talking, and driving—a battery-powered toy go-kart, that is.

No matter, he was always in motion. "He was rowdy," Pattie says of the first of the family's three children (son Austin was born in 1982 and daughter Montgomery Lee in 1985). "He was always wanting to do something. He didn't sit and play with toys. He ran. He jumped. He wasn't easy to go places because he was busy. He was into everything. He always wanted to be with his

dad. It was always go, go, go!"

Although surrounded by racing, Adam's interest moved toward horses, his mother's first love. He took riding lessons when he was about five years old and later showed horses in a few area events.

Among the keepsakes the family has is a note Adam wrote when he was about seven years old. "I'm going to be a jockey someday." The dream didn't last. He was almost too big then. While he was as thin as a two-by-four in his late teens, that came only after shedding more than forty pounds. With a jockey career fading, Adam's interest in auto racing grew after family friends took him to a go-kart race to watch Archie Kennedy compete.

"I was hooked," Adam said less than two months before his death. "There were kids that were racing at the time. Kids my age. I wanted to be like my daddy at a young age. Seeing seven-year olds doing good and running fast kind of intrigued me."

Kennedy found a go-kart for Adam. Soon they were racing throughout the state, winning some, losing other times, but always having fun. That continued until Adam was twelve years old, when he took a year off from racing, bored with the success he'd had in go-karts. He returned to racing when Felix Sabates, who owned the NASCAR team Kyle drove for at the time, gave Adam a Legends car, which is a smaller version of the jalopies used in the sport's early days.

When Adam was about fifteen, Kyle

PREVIOUS SPREAD ADAM AT ABOUT SIX-WEEKS OLD TOP LEFT PLAYING TOP RIGHT FISHING WITH DAD AND HIS BABY BROTHER

bought him a Late Model car, a full-bod-ied car raced on local short tracks across the country. Kyle told Adam, "You build it, you race it."

Adam worked on it for about two weeks and then quit. Months later, Adam began working on it and got some help from friends. He was ready to race it when he was sixteen.

Nothing interested Adam more than racing. He spent most of his free time at the race shop that housed his car, leaving little time for schoolwork.

"He wasn't a good student," Pattie says. "He wasn't an intellect. Anymore to be a good student, you've got to be a real intellect these days.

"Adam hated school but didn't lack focus and direction, because he didn't mind how hard he had to work, and he didn't mind what time he had to get up as long as he was doing what he wanted to do.

"I was a teacher. I totally believed in an education—college, master's degree; going on to school—but there are situations where school is just not for every-body, and that doesn't mean you're a fail-ure. That's the story behind Adam. Just because school is not your thing ... that doesn't mean you're a failure."

While school wasn't for Adam, he was always relaxed at home and in the room he shared with Austin. They never had separate rooms. Kyle and Pattie planned for their home to be a guest house but it never was. Instead, the family

invested its money in land. Living in cramp quarters mirrored the family's closeness. Although Kyle was gone to races—or, early in his driving career, to concerts as he moonlighted as a country and western singer—the family remained close. Kyle called home several times a day, no matter where he was.

That family bond was passed to the children. With little space in their room, Adam and Austin pushed their twin beds together to make one big bed. Once the lights were out, they would talk. Montgomery Lee, whose bedroom was across a narrow hall from her brothers' room, recalls many nights of Adam's and Austin's voices lulling her to sleep. Even after she slept, the brothers talked. "We would be dragging the next day at school," Austin says of those late-night conversations.

When they were older, Adam often would keep Austin up, but not as much with his talking. "The most memorable thing I can remember about sharing a room with Adam was that he had gotten this computer," says Austin, who shares his father's energy in telling stories not only through voice inflections but with hand movement. "It was a big-screen computer. The only thing he had bought this computer for was a high-tech comput-er game. A NASCAR racing game.

"He would get on this thing at eight o'clock at night and he would set Daytona, Indy, or one of these tracks for 500 laps. He would start racing at eight.

Come midnight he's still racing it, so I would have to fall asleep to him, down-shifting and then him hitting the wall and cussing at the wall because the wall hit him or cussing at other drivers because they jumped out in front of him or cut him off.

"I would try to sleep. I had to be at school the next morning at six o'clock and he would be racing until two o'clock at night."

Always trying to get back to victory lane.

ADAM'S BIRTH DIDN'T JUST MAKE PETTY HEADLINES, BUT WAS THE TALK OF THE TOWN, TOO

DALE INMAN TAUGHT ADAM HOW TO SPIT, WHICH ADAM LATER DEMONSTRATED ON TV

GUMMY ON ADAM'S HORSE, SIMON, THE RESIDENT FENCE-CLIMBING TROUBLEMAKER

SNOW DAY FOR AUSTIN, GUMMY, AND ADAM (LEFT TO RIGHT) **ABOVE RIGHT** EACH YEAR A GRANDCHILD DRAWS RICHARD AND LYNDA'S CHRISTMAS CARD (HERE: 2001'S)

The white pony made for a memorable Christmas in 1986 when Adam was six years old. Thrilled with receiving Suzy, Adam took her out to the field to jump picnic benches and a table he had placed on their side. "He was going around in circles, jumping the bench, table, bench; round; bench, table, bench," Pattie says. "Well, the pony was about to fall over. She was completely giving out. She had done this all day long. The pony is tired, she needs to be put up.

" 'One more time, Mom. One more time!'

"Well, he made one more round and she made the bench and she made the table and she balked on the second bench. You know, they stop, they balk and go the other way, and refuse to jump. So she refused, and he went [off the horse] and he broke his collarbone."

PATTIE'S FAVORITE PICTURE—ADAM AT ONE, IN THE CAR KYLE PUT TOGETHER. ADAM LOVED IT SO MUCH THAT HE WORE DOWN THE REAR WHEELS BY CONSTANTLY SPINNING THEM

98 ADAM AND HIS TRICYCLE

KYLE'S BIGGEST FAN CLUB, ADAM AND AUSTIN, WITH JON WOOD (CENTER), WHOSE FAMILY, THE WOODS BROTHERS, OWNED THE TEAM KYLE DROVE FOR AT THE TIME

FAMILY TIME AT HOME

"Add-Dum." The word stretched and paused but it was evident what Montgomery Lee, Kyle and Pattie's youngest child, was saying with her first word. It was only fitting that she said her oldest brother's name first instead of Momma or Daddy.

Montgomery Lee and Adam enjoyed a special bond. She hated her car seat and was not content unless she rode in Adam's lap, facing him. It gave her more chances to look at his face.

Montgomery Lee misses those moments. She prizes the few photographs she has with just her and Adam. There are many photos of the family together but few of just her and Adam because when he was racing, she was showing horses, leading to a path that would make her a world champion.

"When I look at pictures, they always bring a smile to my face because I know what I was doing that day, when we took that picture, why we took that picture," Montgomery Lee says.

Her favorite picture of her and Adam is from when she was about five years old and he was about ten.

She is wearing a white dress and hat. He has on cowboy boots. As they sit on the grass, a pony can be seen in the background, sticking its head through the fence to eat the grass.

"I keep it in my Bible," Montgomery Lee says of the photo. "Every problem I have, that's where I go to first. As soon as I open my Bible, the first thing I see is a picture of my brother."

superswappers

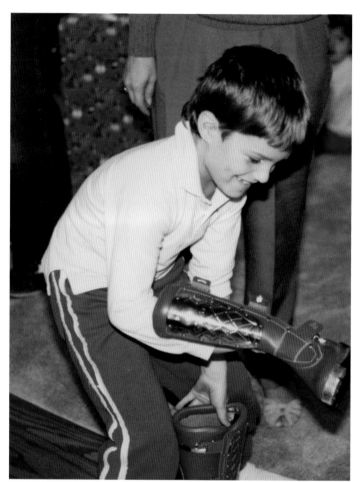

ALL-AROUND ATHLETE, FROM SOCCER TO SKIING, AND EVEN MOTORCYCLING

ADAM'S INTEREST IN RACING BEGAN WITH GO-KARTS

ADAM WITH HIS DRIVING INSTRUCTOR

DRIVING SCHOOL, 1990s

Fathers and Sons

FATHERS AND SONS

Adam didn't need to look far for a role model growing up. He had his father. "My dad was always real close to us even though during the early years he was gone a lot," Adam said in late March 2000, sitting at the family's kitchen table next to his mom, as outside, geese flew over the pond and horses grazed on the Petty farm. "He would always take time to come home and be with us. He helped us work on our go-karts. When he had time, he would go to the go-kart race. I wanted to be like Dad."

To be like the man who plucked the guitar and sang to his young children about taking baths or a belly-button monster or some other song made up as he played. Like the man whose compassion touched those less fortunate through gifts of money or time. Like the man who guided Adam's racing career.

At the track. At home. At the motor home. When their schedules didn't pull them apart, they often were together. Talking, joking, and relaxing.

"We're together so much that we're more like best friends," Adam said a few days before his Winston Cup debut in April 2000 at Texas Motor Speedway. "I feel like I can go tell him anything." While blood made them father-son, their bond was stronger. After Adam's death, Kyle said how difficult Thursday nights were for him. That often had been the night Kyle and Adam spent the most time together at the racetrack. Adam would

have arrived at the track earlier in the day to be with his crew, and Kyle arrived that night for the next day's track action. They talked racing, life, and anything else two friends might discuss. Other times they didn't have to say much. Just being together was what made those times so special.

As they spent more time together, their mannerisms melded. Adam would say "10-4, 10-4" on the radio when he finished a conversation with his crew chief, just as his father does. Their conversations often were a series of action sequences, from hands and arms climbing and falling to heads pivoting and bodies rocking. They both liked to tease close friends. Just when they had somebody flustered, they would say, "I'm just picking on ya," followed by that big Petty grin.

It wasn't just time at the track that was meaningful for both. Adam wanted to be with his dad whenever he could.

"Adam didn't go to dinner or lunch until he saw where his dad was going to dinner or lunch," Pattie says. "He started early, early in the morning. 'Where do you want to eat lunch, Dad? Where do you want to eat lunch? He hadn't but got back to work from lunch and he's calling, 'Where are we eating supper?' Everything he did always included Dad and us. Kyle tried to let him do things on his own but [Adam] didn't want that. He just wanted to be right with his dad."

He often followed his father's advice, even about such things as autographs.

PREVIOUS SPREAD ADAM SAID HE WANTED TO BE LIKE HIS FATHER, AND WAS MOVING CLOSER TO THAT GOAL EACH DAY
TOP LEFT KYLE, RICHARD, AND SHARON
TOP RIGHT ADAM AND KYLE

When Adam started signing autographs, his signature was a maze of loops, lines, and letters hard to decipher. Kyle told him a signature was worthless if a fan couldn't read it. Adam's script soon became easier to read.

After more than twenty years as a driver of Winston Cup racing, and a lifetime around the sport, time together invigorated Kyle.

"When you're around this thing for so long, it's just like anything, you get jaded," Kyle says. "It's always exciting to take people to a race for the first time, because you've gone nine million times and they see things for the first time. I think that's the way going to the racetrack with Adam was. He saw things for the first time, even though he had been around racing for a lot of years.

"He appreciated the Goodyear guys mounting tires for him. He appreciated the fans asking for his autograph. He appreciated [media] asking him for interviews and stuff because it was all new to him. He was still at that stage where he appreciated people doing things for him. From that aspect, you looked at the sport a little different. It did make you appreciate all the things and all the people that make everything work."

Adam valued his father's work on his team. Adam often told his dad to focus more on his own team. While some might have given their son a team and said "there you go," Kyle tried to give Adam every bit of help.

"The way I look at things, it doesn't make any difference how you get there if the end result is still the same," Kyle says. "Adam wanted to be a Winston Cup driver. You can make it hard on him and he's probably still going to be a Winston Cup driver, or you can make it easier and he's going to end up a Winston Cup driver faster, and hopefully better, because you've given him better stuff and better tutelage."

Kyle says he was just trying to do what many parents might do.

"Your parents do the best they can for you," Kyle says, "and then you do the best you can."

KYLE HAS SAID THAT HIS FAMILY IS SIMILAR TO FARMERS. IT'S JUST THAT THE
PETTYS HAVE BEEN AROUND RACING FOR YEARS AND THAT'S ALL THEY KNOW
HERE RICHARD WITH KYLE AT NORTH WILKESBORO

ADAM REACHING THROUGH A FENCE TO KYLE, AT DAYTONA

Richard admires the relationship Kyle and Adam had. When Richard grew up, his father, Lee, was a no-nonsense person who kept his children busy. Richard admits he was too busy to spend as much time as he would have liked with Kyle as Kyle grew up. One senses the pride Richard has in how Kyle and Adam related to each other. "There has never been a prouder parent than what Kyle was," Richard says. "Kyle and Adam were very, very close. Kyle and myself, under the way I grew up, the way he grew up with me having to do the business and stuff, we're probably closer now than we've ever been, except when he was real little.

"We still don't have the click that Adam and Kyle had. They were like brothers. Close brothers. It wasn't like a father-son operation. They were very, very close. It had to be really, really, really tough on Kyle, because Kyle had looked at it and put his career and Petty Enterprises all on Adam.

"He had confidence in him. He had seen the ability in him, and he was going to do everything he could, no matter how much it hurt Kyle's career or no matter what he had to sacrifice; he was doing it for Adam."

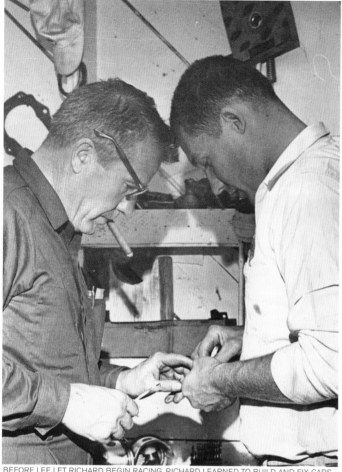

BEFORE LEE LET RICHARD BEGIN RACING, RICHARD LEARNED TO BUILD AND FIX CARS

STRAIGHT: KYLE POINTS THE WAY FOR RICHARD

LEE, RICHARD, AND KYLE

Jason Jarrett was surprised to hear the voice on the phone. "One or two weeks after I won at Kansas," Jarrett says of his first career ARCA series victory in 2001, "I was sitting in my house and my cell phone rings. It was Kyle. 'Man, I just wanted to call and congratulate you on your win.' I was so shocked, I didn't even know what to think. That made my week."

Jarrett, whose grandfather Ned and father, Dale, are both former NASCAR champions, knew the Pettys from his days of playing with Adam, and other children of drivers at race tracks, while their fathers raced.

"I probably look up to [Kyle] as much as I do anybody," Jarrett says. "For doing things like that and doing all the stuff he's done for charity. There's a lot more to racing and being a good person than just winning races."

Jarrett saw Kyle's influence on Adam. "Kyle's always been very compli- mentary," Jarrett says. "When you do something good, he tells you. When you do something bad, he has a nice way of saying, 'Hey, maybe you need to do it this way.' I think that's probably why they got along good. He knew what the pressure was like. He was right there with Adam to help him deal with it."

FOUR GENERATIONS TOGETHER: **LEFT TO RIGHT** KYLE, ADAM, LEE, AND RICHARD

TRACK TIME TOGETHER, AS CONFIDANTS AND BEST FRIENDS

THE UPS AND DOWNS OF LIFE. ADAM AND KYLE ENGAGE IN WHAT PATTIE CALLS "A DISCUSSION" OUTSIDE THE PETTY ENTERPRISES OFFICE **BELOW** KYLE WATCHES OVER ADAM AND HIS CAR

A CHAT AT THE TRACK

CHARLOTTE, 1998: PROUD DAD

Kyle fidgeted on pit road. Standing. Sitting. Moving. He wasn't used to watching his son race on such a big track when Adam made his Automobile Racing Club of America debut on September 30, 1998, at the 1.5-mile raceway then known as Charlotte Motor Speedway.

Richard stood next to car owner Felix Sabates on the balcony of the condominiums outside Turn 1. Every so often, Richard tugged on Sabates's earphones. "Look at this! Look at that!" Richard shouted to Sabates as they watched Adam take the lead, doing what Lee, Richard, and Kyle have done.

"I've never seen [Richard], before or after, do something like that," Sabates said.

Adam's brief racing career provided special moments on and off the track. Few events meant as much to the family as that ARCA race since so many of them were at the track, which is about an hour's drive from their homes.

Pattie stood atop the family's motor home in the infield behind the garage, joined by friends jumping up on the roof as Adam raced with the lead. Austin stood with her, while Montgomery Lee was in the motor home doing homework. She tried to complete an assignment due the next day, but she didn't finish it in time because of that night's excitement.

Adam took the lead for good with

sixteen laps left. With five laps left, Austin ran toward the team's pit, reaching it just as his big brother crossed the finish line one-tenth of a second ahead of runner-up Mike Wallace.

Thus began the sprint to the winner's circle. Richard hopped on a moped and sped toward the celebration, displaying the zest for speed that remains despite having retired as a driver in 1992. The rest of the family ran. They were there when Adam emerged from the car; he sprayed everyone with a soft drink and embraced his father in a bear hug.

"I swear I thought Dad and Mom and Montgomery Lee and everybody was about to cry," Austin says.

"That's just one of those times that you just think that life is so good," says Lynda, Richard's wife and Adam's grandmother, who is so familiar with victory lane celebrations.

Adam had won races before. He won his first ASA race three months earlier when he came back from two laps down. That victory came in Odessa, Missouri, and there wasn't any family there. When Adam called Kyle from victory lane that night, Kyle first thought Adam had finished in the top three.

This time, Adam, two months past his eighteenth birthday, won before family and friends. He became ARCA's youngest winner on a superspeedway, breaking the record held by Kyle when he won in 1979 at Daytona in his series debut.

"The part I remember is how much

fun he seemed to have and how happy everybody was in victory lane," Kyle says, sitting in an office at Petty Enterprises, a few hundred feet from where that winning car sits in the Richard Petty Museum, still crinkled around the rear bumper where Adam backed into the wall in a crash during practice.

Less than three weeks later, Adam made his Busch Grand National debut, starting eleventh and finishing twenty-seventh at Gateway International Raceway in Madison, Illinois, the first of three races he started that year.

Although he didn't win in the season-opening Busch Grand National race at Daytona in February 1999, many of that day's emotions mirrored those of the ARCA victory.

Adam finished sixth in his first race at the historic 2.5-mile track where his great-grandfather had won, his grandfather had won, and his father had won.

Dale Inman, who won series titles as Richard's crew chief, was Adam's spotter that day, standing on the press-box roof and alerting Adam to potential problems in front or beside him. Inman called it one of his highlights in a lifetime spent in racing.

Many others were just as pleased after the race. None more so than Adam.

"I just remember the smile," says Mark Mauldin, who was on Adam's pit crew that year. "You never forget that big ol' smile he had. I can remember seeing him climb out, and that big grin."

After Adam exited the car, he saw his friend Archie Kennedy, who had served as Adam's racing tutor when the youngster raced go-karts. On this day, Kennedy worked on Adam's pit crew. "He said, 'I remember everything about Liberty,'" Kennedy recalls as Adam referred to the North Carolina go-kart track where they often raced. "At Liberty you drafted; two cars were faster than one. He said that was what he was thinking about the whole time out there when he was running with people. He was concentrating on drafting, just like he had done over here at Liberty." The only difference was that instead of go-karts, Adam was driving a 3,300-pound red, purple, and green stock car at more than 190 mph. That race would be one of his best of the season. Adam finished his rookie year with four top-ten finishes in twenty-nine starts and placed third in the rookie of the year points standings.

Results aside, Adam became as well known to many in the garage area for his bubble gum habit. Although he rarely ate sweets (except Lucky Charms cereal, which he ate at all hours), Adam chewed bubble gum. It had to be the individually wrapped pieces. As soon as the gum lost its flavor, he spit it out and chewed more, leaving wrappers and gum all over. The transporter that hauled his cars and the team's equipment from race to race had a one-gallon bucket for his gum, and crew member Stephen Mitchell says it wasn't uncommon for the bucket to be refilled at least once each race weekend.

"Any time anyone stepped in bubble gum they would immediately come to Adam," says Chris Hussey, who was Adam's crew chief late in the 1999 season and in 2000 and who once had the back of his car littered with bubble gum wrappers after Adam rode with him to Bristol. "If they stepped in bubble gum on the other side of the racetrack, they would come to Adam and blame it on him because that was their joke with him. That got to be the running thing in the Busch Grand National garage."

Jokes or wins, people often were smiling when they were around Adam.

A TYPICAL SCENE: ADAM GETTING ADVICE FROM THE KING. AS USUAL, ADAM IS CHEWING A WAD OF GUM

CALM AND COOL ADAM

DALE EARNHARDT JR AND MATT KENSETH (LEFT AND CENTER) GOOFIN' WITH ADAM BEFORE A TV INTERVIEW

ADAM'S ARCA CELEBRATION AT CHARLOTTE, SEPTEMBER '98: STILL GETTING ADVICE FROM THE KING, EVEN AFTER HE WON!

ARCA VICTORY LANE: FRIENDS HAD TO SEW THE PATCHES ON ADAM'S UNIFORM MINUTES BEFORE THE RACE AFTER FINDING OUT SAFETY PINS WEREN'T ALLOWED

WAVING TO THE WINSTON CUP DRIVERS AFTER FINISHING THE BUSCH RACE IN DAYTONA, 1999

PACKING UP IN THE RAIN AT THE NC SPEEDWAY

SIX YEARS OF BRACES SURE PAID OFF!

SPEEDING TO ARCA VICTORY–CHARLOTTE, SEPTEMBER 1998: "HUMPY" WHEELER (TRACK PRESIDENT) CALLED ADAM'S WIN ONE OF THE TRACK'S MOST MEMORABLE MOMENTS

DAYTONA WAS ONE OF ADAM'S FAVORITE TRACKS. AFTER YEARS OF GOING THERE TO WATCH, HE GOT HIS CHANCE TO RACE IT IN FEBRUARY 1999—AT JUST EIGHTEEN YEARS OLD!

A LITTLE R&R AFTER HIS FIRST DAYTONA RACE (HE CAME IN SIXTH)

"He was so funny," fellow competitor Hank Parker Jr. says while laughing about Adam. They often picked on each other, trying to outdo one another. "He was always the first one to be laughing and say something, but he was the shyest person around a girl that I ever met.

"He wanted to go out with my sister. I just didn't let anybody go out with my sister. He was such a good guy, and he was so shy I had nothing to worry about. I told him I wouldn't say anything to her about it: 'I'll tell you what I'll do, I'll just introduce you to her at the racetrack or something. I won't say anything about it.'

"We were testing at Charlotte. I called my sister. So she came by and we're hanging out in the trailer, and I see Adam standing there, so I say, 'Hey, I want to introduce you to somebody.' She's like, 'OK.'

"I walk over there," Parker says as his laughter interrupts the story, "and say, 'Adam, this is Lucy, my sister, and Lucy, this is Adam. He has a crush on you and wants to go out with you.'

"He was so embarrassed. He was punching me. 'Man, what are you doing?' "

Parker is nearly doubled over, laughing. "That was really funny."

BELOW A GOOD LUCK HUG FOR HER BIG BROTHER (AND ONE OF GUMMY'S FAVORITE PICTURES)

THUMBS UP FROM THE KING AT THE DAYTONA BUSCH RACE, FEBRUARY 1999

MORNING, NOON OR NIGHT, IT DIDN'T MATTER, ADAM ATE CEREAL AT
ANY TIME OF THE DAY

FAMILY AT THE TRACK, 1999

"I can tell you this one story, which in my heart is an awesome story," says Seth Jenkins with a wide grin under his Number 45 cap.

Jenkins first met Adam in a physical education class at Randleman High School, became friends, and now works at Petty Enterprises for the Number 44 team with driver Buckshot Jones. "We went to the movies one night. I think it was just me and him, and it was a later movie. We got back late. It was like twelve o'clock or whatever. We stayed up a while watching TV. He was like, 'Seth, we need to get to bed.' I said, 'Come on, it's Friday night. Come on, we can sleep in, it's Saturday.'

"No. He said, 'You're going to set that alarm clock for five o'clock. I've got to get up.'

" 'We're not getting up at five o'clock. Tomorrow is Saturday.' Little did I know he set the alarm clock for five o'clock. I hear his alarm clock go off. I jump up. I'm mad. I was like, 'Adam, what are you doing?'

"He was like, 'I've got to get up to go to the race shop.'

"I thought, 'No big deal.' He was just playing around. He'll just probably go home and go to bed. I set the alarm clock for an hour later. I just thought, 'I'm going to sneak over there and see what he's doing.' So I sneak over on him, and he was in there working on his Late Model car by himself.

"I just think of that story all the time. 'I know I can accomplish anything if I just work at it'—that's his attitude."

KYLE'S PRESENCE OUTSIDE ADAM'S CAR WAS MORAL SUPPORT FOR HIM

ADAM RACING IN THE "CRAYON" CAR (FAMILY NICKNAME FOR THE SPREE'S BRIGHT COLORS)

Competitive Drive

The first time he drove beside his father in a Winston Cup race, Adam, grinning at the thought, said he just might have to wave. He looked forward to that moment as he prepared to make his first NASCAR Winston Cup start on April 2, 2000, at Texas Motor Speedway.

While new for Adam, racing against Dad was common for the Pettys. Richard had experienced that moment when he first raced against his father. Maurice raced against Richard and Lee. Kyle got his chance to race against Richard. Texas would be Adam's opportunity to race against his father.

Fathers and sons off track, competitors on track.

But it didn't happen. And Adam never got a second chance.

While his debut proved momentous, emotions ranging from grief to delight wracked the family's weekend.

Lee was in a Greensboro, North Carolina, hospital at the time, where family members maintained a vigil. He had been hospitalized for nearly two months after surgery for a stomach aneurysm. He died three days after the Texas race.

Adam gave the family reason to smile. His debut trumpeted the Petty name, as he became the first fourth-generation driver to compete at the sport's highest level. As Lee's time was ending, Adam showed that the Petty name and its racing business had a bright future.

In a sport that had Dale Earnhardt, Jeff Gordon, and Rusty Wallace, among others, Adam Petty stood out that weekend. He, Kyle, and Stephen Patseavouras, who helped with Adam's public relations, arrived in Fort Worth six days before the race for promotional appearances in anticipation of the accomplishment. Normally, drivers arrive no more than three days before a race. This was special. It was evident on the plane trip to Texas and as Kyle and Adam were chauffeured throughout Fort Worth. They needled each other as they often did, but Patseavouras recalls Kyle trying to make more moments light with witty comments or little jokes so the pressure didn't overcome Adam.

"I think they were both equally excited," Patseavouras says of the father and son's emotions heading into that weekend. "I think Kyle was probably more excited for Adam to finally be at that level."

Everything started well when Adam qualified thirteenth in the forty-three-car field on Thursday for the Busch Grand National race, a companion event that weekend to the Winston Cup race. That day Adam explained what the weekend meant.

"This is something that our family's looked forward to and something I've looked forward to," he said. "I can't believe this is happening when I'm 19 years old."

The next day was not as good.

"I just remember it being hectic and devastating at the same time," Pattie says

134

of the weekend. "We knew when Kyle and Adam went out to practice that they both weren't going to make it."

Adam qualified thirty-third in the Winston Cup car. Kyle was forty-fourth. Only the top twenty-five were guaranteed a starting spot after that first round of qualifying. When the second and final round of qualifying was rained out the next day, the fastest thirty-six cars, including Adam, made the field. The final seven spots were provisionals based on car-owner points accumulated to that point in the season. Seven other teams were ranked higher than Kyle, and he missed the race.

"It kind of busts the weekend a little bit," Adam said that day through a meager smile that couldn't mask his disappointment.

"As much as he wanted to start his first Winston Cup race, he wanted to race against his dad," said Chris Hussey, Adam's crew chief.

Hussey spent much of the day keeping Adam focused on racing and not dwelling on Kyle's situation. The Busch Grand National race wouldn't be helpful. A blown engine dumped oil on the track and eight cars, including Adam's, slid and crashed. He finished thirty-ninth, leaving only the Winston Cup race left on his weekend.

Overcast skies that next day did nothing to dampen Adam's enthusiasm.

Kyle and Adam started the day together, making sponsor appearances at the track. Adam was just ready to race. He asked Patseavouras, who accompanied father and son at the appearances, if it was time to leave so that he could get to the garage and check on his car.

While he might have been nervous at Texas, he was too busy enjoying the moment, seeing a crowd of more than 220,000 fill the stands. Also ready to go was his crew, who gathered around the car for a group photo. They lacked only one thing: Adam. "It was a zoo trying to run him down at the beginning of the race, because we were trying to get our picture in front of the car and he's over there doing this and doing that," says Patseavouras of the pre-race interviews Adam did. "We were kind of like, "Get over here and get a picture with us so we have something to remember this by." "

Kyle gave each team member a framed copy of that photo for Christmas that year.

Few were as proud of Adam's Winston Cup debut as Archie Kennedy, who had driven go-karts with Adam for about five years. Kennedy was on pit road as a member of Petty Enterprises team-mate John Andretti's pit crew that day. Little kept Kennedy's attention away from Adam, though. "I watched every lap he ran before his motor blew," Kennedy says. "I watched him pass people, I watched him get passed, and he handled it very professionally. He might not have been running up front, but he was driving just like everybody else out there. You couldn't tell he hadn't been driving a Winston Cup car."

Just past a third of the way through the 500-mile race, danger appeared. Elliott Sadler was injured when a cut left-rear tire sliced through the car and slapped his shoulder. The Wood Brothers team, which Kyle had driven for in the 1980s, asked him to be the relief driver. Adam knew his father might get into the race. The Wood Brothers couldn't find Kyle, so Hussey, knowing that Pattie was listening to the team's frequency, announced on the radio that Kyle's services were needed. Adam never said anything on the radio about it, but one can only imagine his hope that he would soon see his dad on the track.

Kyle was getting ready to go into the race when Adam's engine quit, ending his day. Shortly after Adam's car coasted into the garage area, Kyle drove onto the track. "I thought my dream was going to come true there for a minute," Adam said about driving with his dad that day. "It would have been fun."

Instead, he looked back at that moment with disappointment. On the flight home in the team plane, crew chief Chris Hussey tried to lift his young driver's spirits. "Man, you just went through the biggest weekend of your career," Hussey told Adam. "But just remember, regardless of the results, it's also the beginning of your career, and you've just got a long, long way to go. So keep your head up, and do everything like you did this weekend and everything will be good."

NOT JUST WORK HAPPENS ON THE TRACK. FAMILY REUNIONS WERE LOOKED FORWARD TO EVERY SUNDAY, 1984

KYLE TRAILS HIS DAD AT NORTH WILKESBORO IN 1991

Kyle had never been to an autograph session like this.

Both he and Adam were at a Fort Worth, Texas, Sprint store five days before Adam's Winston Cup debut. Shortly after they arrived, the black skies turned green, rain fell, and the wind swirled. Yet the line of people waiting to meet both drivers snaked out the store. Few moved for shelter, even after a tornado warning was issued. Kyle recalls the police telling everyone to find cover.

Those in the store remained. Others outside were allowed into another building. "We're in that back room and water is coming through the bottom of the door there and the sirens are going off in the street," says Stephen Patseavouras, who accompanied Kyle and Adam to the store. "We're all back there wondering, 'What in the world are we doing?' Amid the confusion, the Pettys kept signing.

"We were sitting around a desk," Kyle says. "We were still signing pieces of paper so they could go out and give them to those people, the people that were still in there."

A tornado struck downtown Fort Worth, about a few miles from the store, damaging buildings and knocking out several windows of high-rise buildings. "That's as close as a bad storm has come to where we were at, bad enough to mess things," Kyle says.

ADAM CONTINUED THE FAMILY TRADITION WITH HIS FIRST AND ONLY WINSTON CUP START AT TEXAS, IN APRIL 2000

ADAM TOASTING TO HIS ROOKIE RUN AT DAYTONA IN 1999. PATTIE COULDN'T BE PROUDER OF HIS SIXTH-PLACE FINISH

ADAM AND KYLE BEFORE QUALIFYING AT TEXAS, APRIL 2000

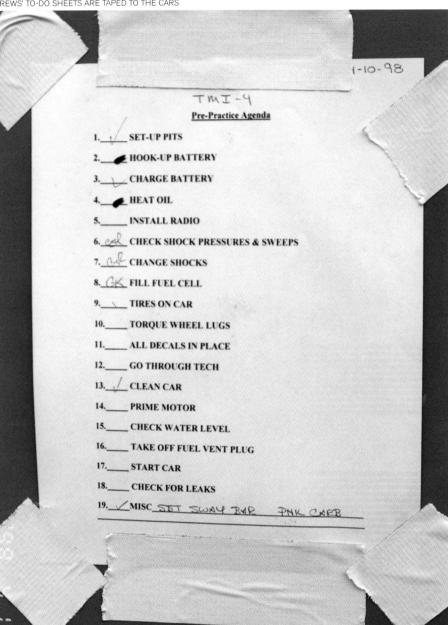

1-10-98

TMI-4

Pre-Practice Agenda

1. ✓ SET-UP PITS
2. ✓ HOOK-UP BATTERY
3. ✓ CHARGE BATTERY
4. ✓ HEAT OIL
5. _____ INSTALL RADIO
6. cal CHECK SHOCK PRESSURES & SWEEPS
7. cal CHANGE SHOCKS
8. GK FILL FUEL CELL
9. _____ TIRES ON CAR
10. _____ TORQUE WHEEL LUGS
11. _____ ALL DECALS IN PLACE
12. _____ GO THROUGH TECH
13. ✓ CLEAN CAR
14. _____ PRIME MOTOR
15. _____ CHECK WATER LEVEL
16. _____ TAKE OFF FUEL VENT PLUG
17. _____ START CAR
18. _____ CHECK FOR LEAKS
19. ✓ MISC SET SWAY BAR PNK CARB

(141)

A TEAM SHOT MOMENTS BEFORE ADAM'S FIRST WINSTON CUP START, APRIL 2000

ADAM (NUMBER 45) RACES IN THE PACK AT TEXAS IN HIS CUP DEBUT. HE WAS MOVING UP FROM
HIS THIRTY-THIRD STARTING SPOT BEFORE HIS MOTOR BROKE DURING THE RACE, APRIL 2000

THE HIGHS AND LOWS OF RACING. ADAM RELAXES WITH HIS CREW

MANY SAW RICHARD WHEN THEY SAW ADAM, BUT IN THIS PICTURE, PATTIE SAYS
SHE SEES KYLE WHEN SHE LOOKS AT ADAM'S EYES

ROCKINGHAM, 1999: ADAM COVERS HIS FACE AFTER FAILING TO MAKE THE
STARTING LINEUP DUE TO RAIN

BEFORE EVERY RACE, PATTIE WOULD LEAN IN AND TELL ADAM, "YOU CAN DO IT, DUFFY MOON," AND ADAM WOULD ALWAYS RESPOND, "I CAN DO IT, DUFFY MOON." DUFFY MOON WAS A CHARACTER THAT ACCOMPLISHED MUCH THROUGH POSITIVE THINKING IN A 1976 ABC AFTERSCHOOL SPECIAL THAT ADAM LIKED

As the start of each race approaches, drivers walk through the garage area and the pits to a stage, often at the start/finish line, for pre-race introductions. That walk is one of the last times for drivers to spend with friends and family. Many walk with their wife. Those not married often walk with their girlfriend, while others walk alone, preparing for the race.

Adam walked with Pattie. "I can remember saying, 'Adam, you don't want me to walk to your race car with you,' " Pattie says. "I would say, 'I'll catch up with you. I don't have to walk with you.'

"He went, 'I want you to walk with me.' I can remember how good that made me feel." "I can remember saying, 'I don't want them to think you

have to be with your mom.' He said, 'I really don't care. You're the best-looking woman here.'

"It was so special that he would say those things, because it was really sweet."

Just because Adam was making his Winston Cup debut at Texas didn't mean he was going to change the routine.

"I can remember in Texas going, 'Listen, you are a Winston Cup driver, I'm not walking out with you, I'll catch up to you,' " Pattie says.

"He said, 'You better walk out with me.' "

They did.

NEWS & RECORD

Greensboro, North Carolina

Heir to Petty dynasty dies

IMPACT

Kyle looks at pictures fans send of him and can tell if the photo was taken before or after Adam's accident, although Kyle's goatee and ponytail remain. "When I see a photo of myself with earrings in, I know it happened pre–May 12, 2000," Kyle says. "Since that time, I don't have them; then I know it's after Adam's accident.

"When Mike [Helton, NASCAR's president] called me when we were in England and told me about Adam's accident, then I think from one minute to the next I wasn't a kid anymore. So it was time to take your earrings out. That was a kid thing. All of a sudden, I was forced to have to grow up because I had never. I had just floated. I wasn't a kid, and it was time to grow up and do something different."

In different ways, different people were affected by Adam's death, including a couple that reunited, in part, due to him.

Montgomery Lee honks the horn every time she goes under the Interstate 40/85 underpass on Greensboro Road, in Greensboro, North Carolina. It's a personal tribute to her older brother and reminder of the night the Petty children went on a triple date together to a restaurant. On the way, the boy Montgomery Lee was with asked Adam to honk the horn when they went under the bridge. It's just another way to keep Adam's memory fresh.

His memory also carries on in a reunited couple. His accident brought former driver Bobby Allison and his wife, Judy, back together. The couple of thirty-six years endured the deaths of their two sons—Clifford, in a Busch Grand National crash in 1992, at Michigan, and Davey, from injuries suffered in a helicopter crash at Talladega in 1993. Their divorce a few years later was bitter.

The day of Adam's accident, Bobby and Judy were attending the wedding of Davey's widow, Liz, in Nashville, Tennessee. Understanding the Pettys' grief, Bobby and Judy set aside their differences and went together on the eight-hour drive to the Petty family home. During that trip, the Allisons had the time to speak frankly about their relationship and each other. It started a healing process. At the service celebrating Adam's life, the Allisons held hands as they walked in behind the Pettys. Less than two months later, the Allisons remarried.

"You look at the accident and you look at Bobby and Judy getting together and you look at the people that Adam's life affected—there was a lot of positives that came out of things," Kyle says. Robbie Loomis, crew chief for Jeff Gordon's 2001 championship team, says Adam's accident forced him to reevaluate his priorities in life and racing.

"It's like I told our guys, 'Yes, we want to win races; yes, we want to win championships,' but I said, 'This is life,

PREVIOUS SPREAD AFTER ADAM'S DEATH, KYLE TOOK OVER THE NUMBER 45 CAR
TOP MAY 13, 2000 NEWS HEADLINE

and we've all got to realize that there's a whole lot more out there than just winning races and winning championships,' " says Loomis, who worked at Petty Enterprises for more than a decade before joining Gordon's team in 2000. "Up until that point, I thought we were going to be around forever. When Adam died, that really hit home because I saw everything in place, that Adam was going to be a Winston Cup champion. I saw Petty Enterprises building. I knew how Kyle and his rapport was, and it was like it was all working so good that it had to be destiny, and then all of a sudden it was changed. From that time on then, that really helped me handle the rough times or the bad times.

"My focus was on knowing that there was something a lot greater out there than what we were doing on that given Sunday."

For Pattie, high achievement and danger on the track have always been separate issues, which is how she was able to be a supportive mom, and coach, to Adam.

"I look at it from a perspective that I don't allow the fear factor to come in, I only am concentrated on our performance level," Pattie says. "During a race, you become very anxious for them to do good, you become very anxious for a good finishing position, you are very anxious if there is a problem. You put your fear on the back burner until something on the track does happen. Then, your natural...

emotion of your loved one becomes very evident if there is a wreck."

Pattie wanted those among the crowd of more than 1,000 at the celebration of Adam's life to experience what Loomis did. "I wanted Adam's service to say something to people about his life and how important it was," she says. "We know where we were. Adam knew where he was with the Lord. There was never a question of where he was going."

So she had the song "When All is Said and Done" performed. It was a song she and Adam were listening to one night a few weeks before his accident. As it played, they had discussed death and making the most of life instead of worrying about trivial matters. As they talked, the song was played again on the radio.

"I want you to listen to every word," she told him.

"He looked at me when it ended," Pattie says, "and said," 'You know, Mom, you're so right.' "

ATLANTA, NOVEMBER 1992: RICHARD EXITS THE CAR FOR THE FINAL TIME AFTER HIS 1,177TH AND FINAL
NASCAR WINSTON CUP RACE, WITH ESPN ANNOUNCER DR. JERRY PUNCH BEHIND HIM

STRAPPED IN AND READY TO GO **LEFT** KYLE **TOP RIGHT** RICHARD **BOTTOM RIGHT** ADAM

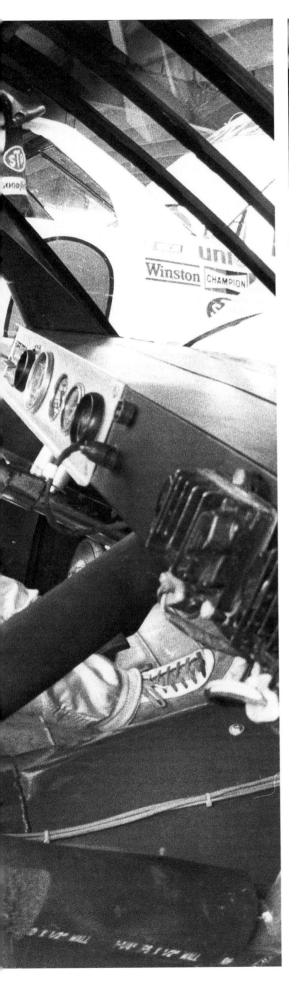

Adam's words are always with Kim Utlaut. She was Adam's sponsor representative at Sprint and traveled to most of his races, from the 1998 season when he competed in the ASA series to his NASCAR Busch Grand National races. That time together left an impression on Utlaut.

"We'd be walking back into the hotel after going to the Outback and we'd be getting ready to go our separate ways, to go to our rooms, and he would say, 'I love you. Thank you for everything,' " she says. "That hits you. That's amazing that a seventeen-year-old, eighteen-year-old, nineteen-year-old can grasp that and articulate his appreciation.

"It made me as an individual realize that I need to do more, whether it's my own family or my own friends, it's OK to say, 'I love you.' We as a society don't do that enough. But Adam did that enough for everybody."

154

WHILE KYLE'S NAME ON HIS CAR DOOR IS IN SCRIPT, ADAM'S IS IN BLOCK LETTERS, AT PATTIE'S REQUEST TO MAKE IT EASIER FOR KIDS TO READ

Although Adam was gone, his brother honored him in the best way he knew. "Mine and his favorite place to eat was Outback [Steakhouse] in High Point," Austin says. "Three nights a week we'd eat there. Chicken on the barbie, extra side of broccoli. That's all he got. There was a time after he died that me and Seth [Jenkins] would go up there and order chicken on the barbie, extra side of broccoli, and they would bring it to the table and it would sit there."

THE FLAGS FLEW AT HALF-STAFF AT PETTY ENTERPRISES

MOURNING AT THE GATES OF THE PETTY FARM

A SPECIAL DECAL CELEBRATING ADAM'S LIFE
WAS GIVEN TO TEAMS

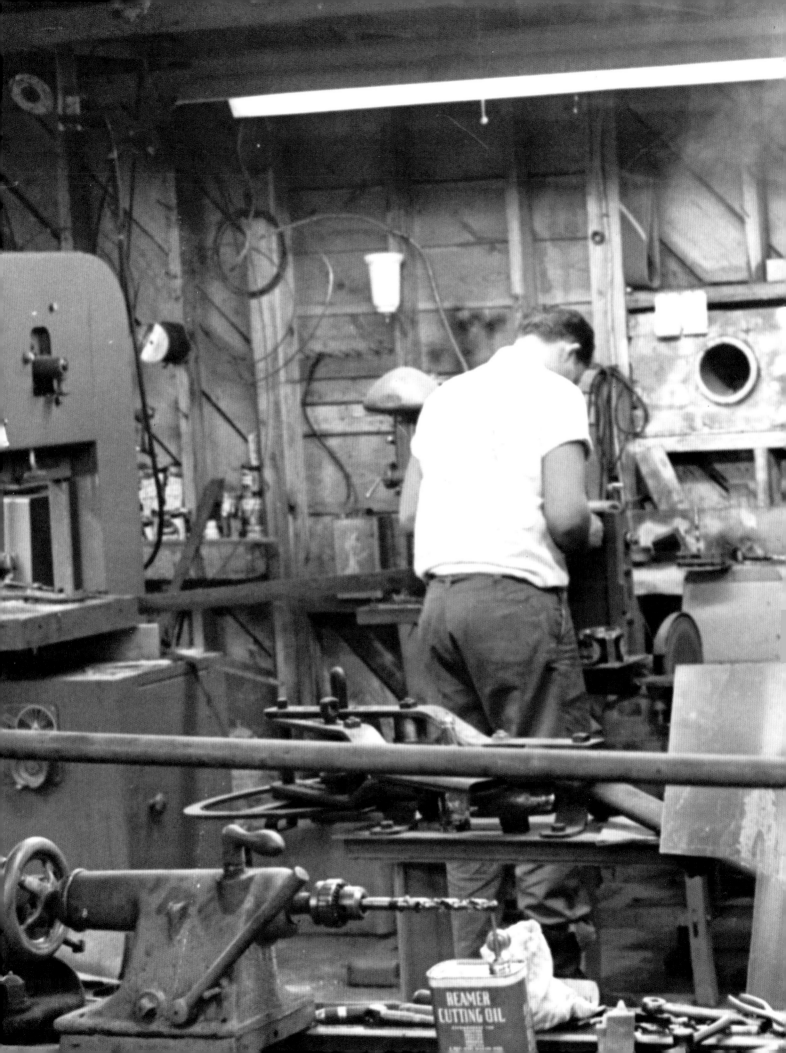

Determination

DETERMINATION

Someday, it would have been his. Just as Richard and Maurice took over the family's race team after Lee backed away, and Kyle took over for Richard, plans were made even before Adam's Winston Cup debut for the day he would run Petty Enterprises.

Although that change will never happen, Kyle continues with the designs he made with Adam in mind.

"I've told these guys in numerous meetings, privately and in front of the whole group," says Kyle, CEO of Petty Enterprises, "that the criteria I use for making changes is that if I look at something and I say, 'If Adam was here driving the car, would that make this car better?' If the answer is yes, then I'm going to make a change. If the answer is no, then I probably won't make a change."

Kyle has followed that code for several years. He left the team owned by Felix Sabates after the 1996 season, when Adam was sixteen, to form his own team so Adam would have a ride if he couldn't get one when he moved to Winston Cup. Two years later, rising costs led to Kyle rejoining Petty Enterprises and merging the teams for a two-car operation and a Busch Grand National car for Adam.

One of the biggest moves came when the team left Pontiac after the 2000 season and joined Dodge, which had been a top competitor through the 1970s before leaving the sport and had a long history with the family.

"When Adam came along, we did everything we could to give him the very best people, the very best cars, the very best engines, the very best stuff that we could give him," Kyle says. "When we started down the road for the Winston Cup stuff, we did the very same thing and that was why we were with Dodge, to give him what we felt like was a leg up with a manufacturer, to start down that road and go do something."

Kyle has said that the Dodge change was just the beginning of a five-year plan that included a change in engine builders and a new team manager entering the 2002 season.

"We went that way and then we got cut off with the accident," Richard says of the five-year plan. "We said, 'We've started that way and that's the way we were going to go. We just go at it from the same angle. It's just going to be different because it's not going to be left to Adam.'"

Maybe so, but Kyle still refers to the Number 45 team as Adam's team and does not sign the Number. 45 with his autograph because he says that's Adam's number, not his. Kyle says he's just a relief driver for that car. It will always be Adam's team.

While Kyle works to help Petty Enterprises once again become one of the sport's top organizations, he works as hard to build the Number 45 team, so he can say that he made Adam's team one of the best.

PREVIOUS SPREAD RICHARD AND LEE WORK IN THE GARAGE NEXT TO THE FAMILY'S HOME; TODAY, PETTY CREW MEMBERS WORK OUT IN THAT SPACE **TOP (LEFT TO RIGHT)** PAST, PRESENT AND FUTURE: RACING IN GREENSBORO; DALE EARNHARDT AND RICHARD RACING; RICHARD; AUSTIN

"This team doesn't have to go win a race," Kyle says. "This team doesn't have to go win a championship. But if this team continues to make improvements and get better and better and get to where it can run in the top five or top ten pretty consistently, then you know you had a team that could win races and that he would have won races with it."

While Kyle continues to race, Adam's death leaves a gap such that someday there might not be a Petty racing in NASCAR. Ever since NASCAR's first season in 1949, a Petty has competed every year—from Lee to Richard to Kyle. Adam's younger brother, Austin, is enticed by racing but he didn't begin his first full season of racing until 2001, when, at age nineteen, he competed in a Legends car. That doesn't mean Austin might not end up with the organization in some form.

"I've always kind of stood back and looked at it, and it was Grandpa and Dad and Adam's thing," Austin says of racing. "I was going to be the different one that became a pilot in the Air Force or played in an orchestra. About the beginning of [2001], I kind of said to myself that I would like to race."

That first race brought him into a new world.

"Granted, it's not a Winston Cup car, it's not even a half of a Winston Cup car, but it's a race car, and you sit in a seat and you stare over a steering wheel and you're buckled into a five-point seat harness where you're limbs are just starting to go numb because they're so tight, and you look at everything the way Adam had looked through it," Austin says. "It made me feel closer to Dad. It made me feel closer to Adam and Grandpa, and it makes me understand a little bit more what they go through every single week."

Seeing Austin show more of an interest in racing doesn't surprise Kyle.

"He keeps gravitating back to, 'Well, I'd like to try to run this car,' or 'I'd like to go with you and learn the business side of it,' " Kyle says. "He keeps gravitating back to what we do. It's no matter how far you get away from it, at the heart of it, all you know is this."

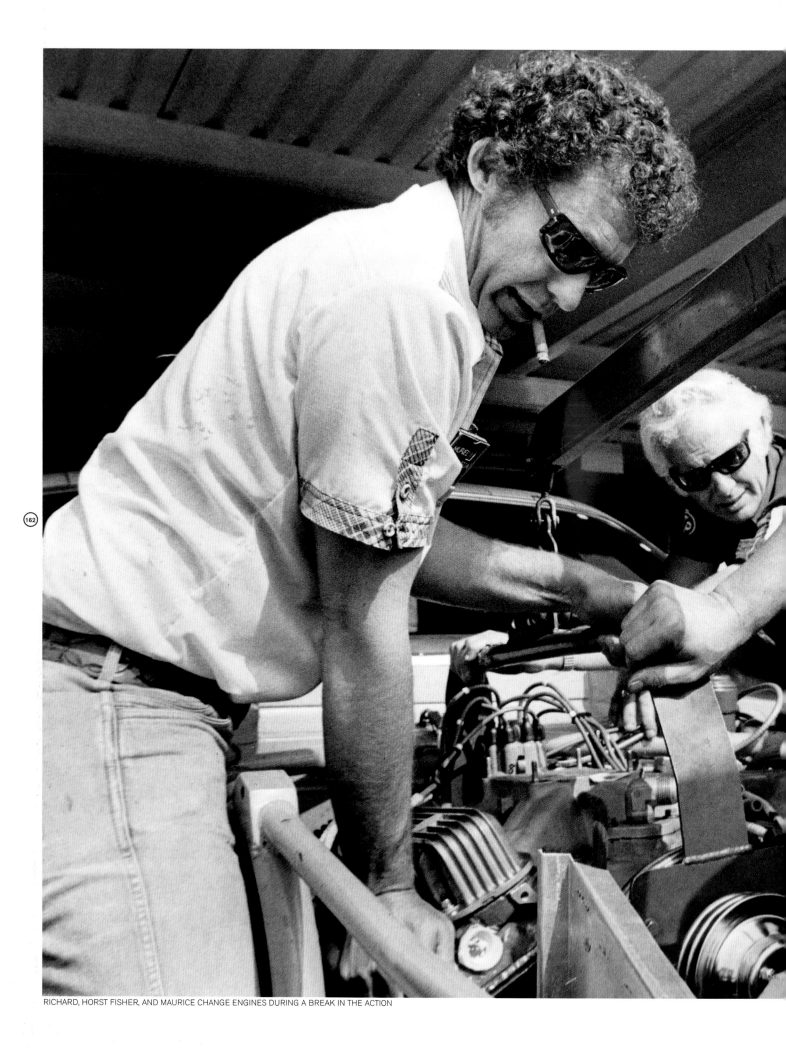

RICHARD, HORST FISHER, AND MAURICE CHANGE ENGINES DURING A BREAK IN THE ACTION

1956: **THIRD FROM LEFT TO RIGHT** MAURICE, LEE, RICHARD, AND DALE WITH CREW TAKING A BREAK AT MARTINSVILLE SPEEDWAY

MAURICE KICKS BACK ON THE HOOD OF RICHARD'S CAR AS KYLE (IN TEAM SHIRT) SITS ON THE BENCH IN THE GARAGE AREA

1963: RICHARD, JIM PASCHAL, JIM HURTUBISE, WHO DROVE IN THREE RACES FOR THE TEAM, AND LEE

ADAM (CENTER) AND HIS CREW DURING HIS LATE MODEL RACING DAYS **ABOVE** RICHARD AND KYLE

Adam always liked the idea of a camp where children with chronic or life-threatening illnesses could go to be children again instead of patients. That such a place wouldn't cost families, burdened by mounting medical bills, appealed even more to him. That was why he encouraged his parents to move forward with the Victory Junction Gang camp before his accident. It is one of the reasons they continued work on the camp after his accident.

"I can remember him asking the same question I did, 'Why does it seem like that kids that are sick tend to come from a family that's already down and out?' " Pattie says. "Why is that?

"He wanted to make a place where, yeah, they may have been sick, but they also got to have a lot of fun, too."

AN EARLY DODGE TEST SESSION AT LOWE'S MOTOR SPEEDWAY IN CHARLOTTE

WHEN NOT ON THE RACETRACK, THE PETTYS AND CREW TINKER WITH THEIR CARS
HERE LEE

MARTINSVILLE, 1949: WORKING ON LEE'S CAR AS RICHARD WATCHES FROM BEHIND

MAURICE

WORKING ON RICHARD'S CAR

Adam will live on in more than memories for siblings Austin and Montgomery Lee. At the service celebrating Adam's life, Montgomery Lee vowed that the first child she has would have Adam's name. Her child will have Adam's middle name, Kyler, because Austin wanted the name Adam for his future child.

"When I lost Adam, I had never lost anybody before, so you always have this thought in the back of your mind that one day you're just going to wake up and not remember anything about him," says Montgomery Lee, who was born in 1985 and was five years younger than Adam. "That scares me. I have that thought a lot. One day I'll forget his voice, or one day I'll forget the way his eyes looked.

"If I name my child something after Adam, I know I'll never forget him, because every time I look at my child I know I'll think about him."

DAY IS DONE: LOADING KYLE'S CAR INTO THE HAULER

IN MEMORY OF ADAM, THE FAMILY KEEPS MANY OF THE CARS HE RACED IN HIS FIRST
SHOP. THE CAR IN THE FRONT LEFT IS FROM TEXAS

Grace and Charity

Kristine Curley never heard the accident.

Adam's public-relations person, who was more the big sister he never had, sat on the inside pit wall at New Hampshire International Speedway on May 12, 2000. Curley didn't need the headphones she wore to muffle the noise from practice. She was focused on a national publication's survey searching for the most giving athletes. Curley had much to tell about Adam and his family.

"The Pettys have a grand tradition of supporting philanthropic causes, from Lee Petty to his son Richard to his son Kyle," Curley wrote, as cars circled on the track. "Now that tradition is being carried on by the newest generation of Pettys in Kyle's son Adam."

Curley wrote about Adam's charitable acts, from visiting sick children to donating money, as his car careened into the Turn 3 wall and he was killed. With that crash, a caring soul, a friend to many, and a kindhearted kid was gone.

"As a father, you're like, 'Man, if only my children could grow up to be like him, it would make me so happy,'" says Bobby Labonte, family friend, NASCAR Winston Cup champion, and father of two children.

Adam's charity work came naturally. He saw his grandfather and father perform various acts including dropping money off at a local homeless shelter to visiting sick children in hospitals across the country. While racing was the family's occupation, charity work was its duty. Kyle credits both his grandmothers for guiding the family's spirit. Friends recount the numerous bake sales, church programs, and school fund-raisers the family participated in through the years.

The sense of service was passed to Richard and Lynda and to their four children—Kyle, Sharon, Lisa, and Rebecca, and their families.

The family's generosity started at home. That's how it was in the first half of the twentieth century. Neighbors looked after neighbors; friends after friends; church members after church members. Soon a community sprouted.

The Pettys were no different. In addition to Level Cross, the Pettys had a second community—those involved with stock-car racing. As racing grew from a regional sport to a national passion, so did the family's dedication to helping others. More communities meant more opportunities to make a difference.

Adam learned that anything he got, he could use to help others. Stephen Patseavouras recalls a time in 1998 when a track owner wanted Adam to come to his facility to race. The track owner asked Patseavouras, who was handling Adam's schedule at the time, what the teenaged driver's appearance fee would be. Patseavouras said $5,000, wondering whether that was too much. The track owner paid it. Adam gave Patseavouras

PREVIOUS SPREAD ADAM'S FINAL CHARITY RIDE WITH KYLE
TOP (LEFT TO RIGHT) ADAM AND KYLE RIDING; RICHARD SIGNING; ADAM AT SPRINT/STARBRIGHT MEDIA EVENT; KRISTINE CURLEY

half the money and donated the other half to a local community group.

Others recall how Adam gave people on the street a few dollars, just as his dad does. Adam also donated his time. He rode on Kyle's annual charity motorcycle ride across the country that ended at the family's farm in Trinity, North Carolina. The weeklong trip included stops at children's hospitals where encouragement, hope, and money were given.

Adam also was a part of the Starbright Foundation, which provided video conferencing for children in hospitals, allowing them to talk to other children who had similar health problems so they didn't feel alone.

Making such trips was not always easy on Adam, especially when he visited children confined to their rooms. Often these were children only a year or two younger than Adam. "I told him, the thing you always have to keep in your mind when you go and see kids is that for some reason that we don't understand and we don't know, they're in this position," Kyle says. "There's nothing they can do about it. They're fighting for their life, where you are just walking through and shaking a hand and saying, 'Hey,' and all this stuff. They may fight for the rest of their life, and it's your job to some degree to look at yourself and say, 'There for the grace of God go I.' That's kind of the way you have to look at it. You have to say, 'I'm incredibly blessed to be standing here beside this bed and not be in the bed.' "

Kim Utlaut, the sponsor representative for Sprint, went to most races with Adam and some hospital visits. She recalls one time when Adam met a cancer patient about two years younger than himself during a Starbright video conference. They both talked about getting their driver's license and traded stories about early driving experiences. Kim said Adam asked her about that patient's welfare from time to time.

The week Adam made his Winston Cup debut at Texas, he asked about that patient but was told the teenager had died. "It really hit Adam hard," Utlaut said. "He saw someone relatively his age that they had shared some time with and some funny stories, and that person was no longer there."

It is those brief encounters that mean so much to people, whether they're meeting Richard, Kyle, or someone else. Richard understood that early. That's why he tried to spend as much time with fans at the track, so much that his crew would start yelling at him because they had packed the car and tools and were ready to leave.

Kyle has that same gift and he shares it often, whether it's sending flowers, as he did about an hour after the birth of crew member Scott Kuhn's child, or offering condolences to an acquaintance for a death in the family. "I don't think it was ever an option, 'Oh, we're not going to do that,' " Kyle says of the family's service toward others. "We weren't raised that way. It's like saying, 'Yes, sir' and 'No, sir' and 'Yes, ma'am' and 'No, ma'am.' You were always raised to do that. I'm forty-one years old and I still have people say, 'You don't have to say, "Yes, sir" to me,' because that's the way that we were raised."

GLEN WOOD (CENTER) AND RICHARD (RIGHT) LEAN IN TO LOOK AS LEE IS WRITING

FANS SURROUND THE PETTYS FOR THEIR SIGNATURES: **TOP** ADAM WITH STEVE PATSEAVOURAS (LEFT) **BOTTOM** RICHARD **OPPOSITE PAGE** KYLE

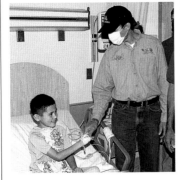

Often a visit from the Pettys proved uplifting for children confined to their hospital room because of their condition. Other times it was not so easy.

"Well, this little boy was evident he was in no condition to talk fun, and he didn't want to talk fun," Pattie recalls of a hospital room visit with Adam during a charity-ride stop one year. "Most of the rooms are very decorated from children that have been there a long time. This room was not very dec-orated. Adam said, 'Well, you haven't been here long, maybe you won't have to stay long.' His mother said, 'Oh, we've been here six years.' Adam in a very coy way said, 'Good, that means you get to go home soon since you've cleaned your walls up.' [The boy] said, 'No, I'll never get to go home.'

"I remember thinking, 'Jeez, what do you say to that?' Adam said, 'Well, you know what? You don't got much stuff on your walls and you think that you're not going home, but miracles happen every day, and we're just going to pray that a miracle happens for you. You know what? You've got your mom here, and I went in those other three rooms and they didn't have anybody. They had lots of pretties on the walls, but their moms weren't there. You're mom is here. I'll bet she's been here every day.' He nodded his head. 'See, I told you that you had something to be thankful for.' "

AUSTIN PERFECTING HIS PENMANSHIP

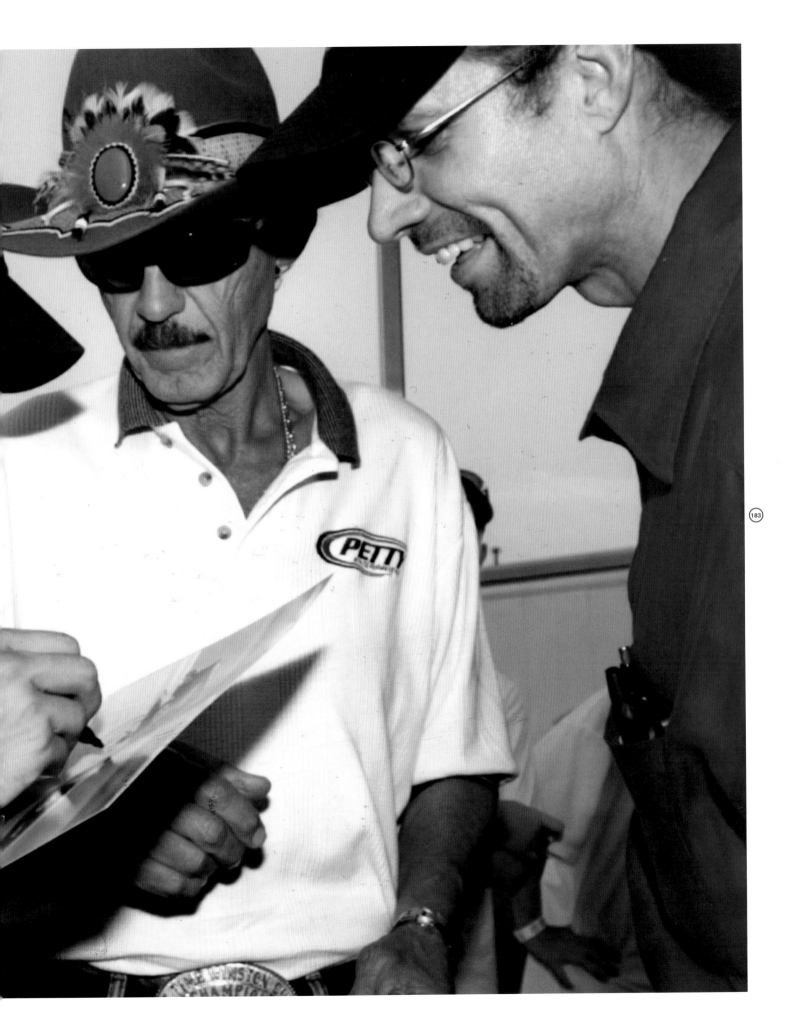

ADAM ADJUSTING TO THE CELEBRITY LIFESTYLE AT AN EARLY AGE AS HE SIGNS FOR HIS AUNT LISA

Family prayers were always important to Adam, no matter if he was on the road or at home. Regardless, each night he would pray with his family.

"Adam was very funny," Pattie says. "He didn't go to bed at night until he said prayers with his family. He literally would not go to bed at night until we all had prayed together. He would get very aggravated with his brother or sister if they were busy or on the computer or doing homework. He was like, 'I have to get to bed, I've got to go to work. We're praying downstairs now!' He's screaming, 'We're praying now!' When the family was at home, they gathered together, often in Kyle and Pattie's bedroom.

"We all started and whoever wanted to say something could say something," Austin says. "Just pray what was on their mind at the moment or if they wanted to pray for somebody or pray for Adam or Dad to be careful at the racetrack. We would do stuff like that."

If Adam was on the road, he would call his parents. "He would call us both if we weren't in the same place," Pattie says. "That was a big thing to him. I think it was testimony he enjoyed telling other people that he still said prayers with his family."

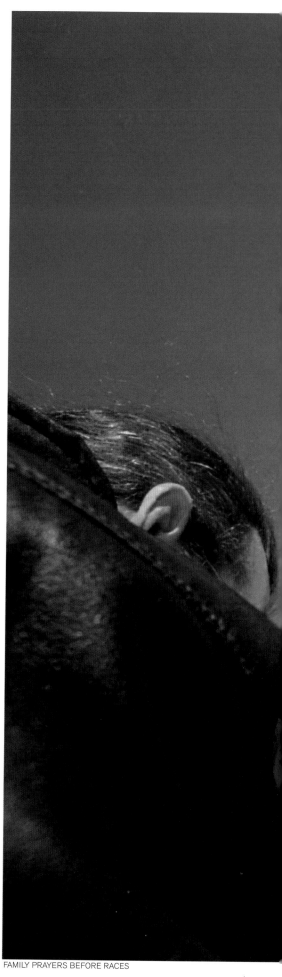

FAMILY PRAYERS BEFORE RACES

1914

1953

1988

1959

1979

1960

CHRONOLOGY

1914
March 14 - Lee Arnold Petty is born.

1937
July 2 - Richard Petty is born to Lee and Elizabeth (née Toomes).

1939
March 27 - Maurice ("The Chief") Petty, Richard's brother and engine builder for most of Richard's career, is born to Lee and Elizabeth.

1949
June 19 - Lee Petty competes in the first NASCAR Strictly Stock race, on a three-quarter-mile dirt track in Charlotte, North Carolina. On lap 107 of the 200-lap event, Petty's car tumbles in Turn 3, ripping off the hood and denting and crinkling the car's roof. Petty suffers only a cut on his cheek.

October 2 - Lee Petty scores the first of his fifty-four career NASCAR victories, winning a 200-lap race on the half-mile dirt track at Heidelberg Speedway in Pittsburgh. Petty earns $1,500.

1954
Lee Petty wins the first of his three Grand National championships.

1958
July 18 - Richard Petty makes his first career NASCAR start, in Toronto. He starts seventh and finishes seventeenth after wrecking on lap fifty-five of the 100-lap event.

Lee Petty wins the second of his three NASCAR championships.

1959
February 22 - Lee Petty, Johnny Beauchamp, and Joe Weatherly cross the finish line three-abreast in the inaugural Daytona 500 on the high-banked track. Beauchamp is sent to victory lane, but photographs a few days later show Petty nipping Beauchamp by about two to three feet. NASCAR rules Lee Petty wins the race.

June 14 - Richard Petty wins his first race with Lee placing second, at Lakewood Speedway in Atlanta. Lee, however, protests. The protest is upheld, and Lee is declared winner and Richard put to second. It was Lee's forty-second career victory.

Lee Petty wins the third of his three NASCAR championships. Richard Petty wins rookie of the year honors.

Richard and Lynda Owens elope, marrying in South Carolina (month and date remain their secret).

1960
February 28 - Richard Petty officially wins his first career NASCAR Grand National race, scoring his victory in a 100-mile race at Charlotte Fairgrounds. Richard wins $800.

June 2 - Kyle Petty is born to Richard and Lynda.

August 3 - Lee Petty and sons Richard and Maurice drive in the same race—the 200-lap race at Dixie Motor Speedway in Birmingham, Alabama, on a quarter-mile track. In the only time all three drive against one another, Richard finishes second, Lee third, and Maurice eighth in the sixteen-car field. This feat was not duplicated until Dale Earnhardt ran against sons Kerry and Dale Jr. in a NASCAR race at Michigan International Speedway in Brooklyn, Michigan, in 2000.

1961
February 24 - Richard Petty is involved in a crash in a qualifying race at Daytona. Richard's car crashes over the wall and goes out of the track. He suffers abrasions and a cut hand. In the second qualifying race that day, Lee Petty is involved in a crash with Johnny Beauchamp, both cars are sent through the guardrail and out of the track. Lee is seriously injured with a punctured lung, multiple fractures of the left chest, a fractured left thigh, a broken collarbone and multiple internal injuries. Although Lee came back to compete in a handful of events, this crash all but ended his career.

June 30 - Sharon Petty, now Sharon Farlow, is born to Richard and Lynda.

1962
June 29 - Timmy Petty is born to Maurice and Patricia.

1964
February 23 - Richard Petty wins the first of his seven Daytona 500s.

Richard Petty wins the first of his record seven NASCAR championships. Lee Petty retires after completing a race at Watkins Glen, New York. Maurice is named Mechanic of the Year.

1974   1979   1998   2000

1979   1991   1998

1965

Outlaw year: Chrysler boycotts first half of season after NASCAR bans its Hemi; the Pettys go drag racing.

September 20 - Lisa Petty, now Lisa Luck, is born to Richard and Lynda.

1966

June 27 - Elizabeth Petty, now Elizabeth Kratzenberg, is born to Maurice and Patricia.

1967

May 13 - Richard Petty wins at Darlington Raceway in Darlington, South Carolina, for his fifty-fifth career victory, passing his father for first place in the category of career victories.

August 12 - Richard Petty wins a race at Bowman Gray Stadium in Winston-Salem, North Carolina, the first of a record ten consecutive victories for Petty, who goes on to win twenty-seven of the forty-eight races he enters that season. He goes on to win his second of seven titles in the greatest season by a driver in NASCAR history. Acknowledging his 1967 streak, the media crowns him "The King."

1968

June 20 - Ritchie Petty is born to Maurice and Patricia.

1969

October 16 - Mark Petty is born to Maurice and Patricia.

1970

May 9 - Richard Petty survives one of his most horrific crashes and one of NASCAR's most famous single-car accidents, at Darlington Raceway in Darlington, South Carolina. Petty's car loses control out of Turn 4, slaps the outside wall, and shoots across the track, hitting the inside wall nearly head-on. The car barrel-rolls seven times. Petty's left arm and shoulder are seen bouncing outside against the car during the crash. The car stops on its roof. Petty suffers only a shoulder injury. Shortly after the crash, NASCAR mandated window nets to keep the drivers inside their cars. Window nets remain today.

1972

STP joins Petty Enterprises as the sponsor of Richard's cars. Richard wins his fourth of seven titles.

1973

May 14 - Rebecca Petty, now Rebecca Moffitt, is born to Richard and Lynda.

1974

Richard Petty wins his fifth of seven Daytona 500s and fifth of seven championships.

1979

February 4 - Kyle marries Pattie Huffman.

Feb. 11 - Kyle Petty makes his driving debut and wins the ARCA race at Daytona.

February 18 - Richard Petty wins his sixth Daytona 500 in spectacular fashion. In the first live broadcast of the race from start to finish, fans watch as leaders Donnie Allison and Cale Yarborough crash on the final lap. Richard Petty, running third, goes on to win after the two wreck and takes the checkered flag as the drivers, joined by Donnie's brother, Bobby, fight near their wrecked cars just off the track in one of racing's most infamous scenes.

Richard Petty wins his seventh and final championship. Richard trailed Darrell Waltrip by two points for the title, but because Richard finishes three spots ahead of Waltrip in the season finale at Ontario Motor Speedway in Ontario, California, he wins the title by eleven points.

1980

July 10 - Adam Kyler Petty is born.

1981

February 15 - Richard Petty wins seventh and final Daytona 500.

1982

March 24- Austin Petty is born.

1984

July 4 - Richard Petty wins his 200th and final NASCAR race, at Daytona, with President Reagan in attendance.

1985

December 17 - Montgomery Lee Petty is born.

1986

February 23 - Kyle Petty wins at Richmond International Raceway in Richmond, Virginia, becoming the first third-generation driver to win a NASCAR race.

1987

Mark and Ritchie Petty, sons of Maurice, make their driving debuts.

1992

Richard Petty's final season as driver.

1995

June 4 - Kyle Petty's earns his eighth and most recent NASCAR victory, at Dover Downs International Speedway in Dover, Delaware.

1998

April 11 - Adam makes his ASA debut at Peach State Speedway in Jefferson, Georgia.

June 2 - Adam wins his first ASA race, capturing victory at I-70 Speedway in Odessa, Missouri. At age seventeen, Adam becomes the series' youngest winner.

September 30 - Adam Petty wins his first ARCA race at Lowe's Motor Speedway in Charlotte. At eighteen years and three months, he becomes the series' youngest winner, eclipsing the mark set by his father at Daytona in 1979 (Kyle was eighteen years and eight months old).

October 17 - Adam competes in his first NASCAR Busch Grand National race, competing at Gateway Raceway in Madison, Illinois.

1999

February 13 - Adam begins his first full season in NASCAR Busch Grand National series by finishing sixth in the season-opening race at Daytona International Speedway.

2000

April 2 - Adam makes his Winston Cup debut at Texas Motor Speedway. A blown engine ends his day early and he finishes fortieth in the forty-three-car field.

April 5 - Lee Petty dies at the age of eighty-six.

May 12 - Adam Petty is killed in a crash during practice at New Hampshire International Speedway.

June 3 - Kyle Petty drives the Number 45 car in the Busch race at Dover Downs International Speedway, and has been driving it ever since.

Front cover: Tom Copeland

Back cover: Bill Livingston

Pages 2-3: ISC Archives

Pages 4-5: Tom Copeland

Pages 6-7: Marvin Gamble/
Kyle and Pattie Family
Collection

Page 8: Top: ISC Archives;
bottom: Richard and Lynda
Family Collection

Pages 10-11 (background):
Tom Copeland

Pages 12-13: News &
Record, Greensboro,
North Carolina

Pages 14: Richard and
Lynda Family Collection

Page 15: Tom Copeland

Page 16: Bill Livingston

Page 17: Kevin Kane

Pages 18-19: Bill Livingston

Pages 20-21: courtesy:
News & Record

Page 22: Left: John Wood;
right: Tom Copeland

Page 24: Lee Petty
Family Collection

Page 25: courtesy:
News & Record

Pages 26-27: Kyle and
Pattie Family Collection

Pages 28-29: Tom Copeland

Pages 30-31: Tom Copeland

Pages 32-33: Tom Copeland

Pages 34-35: Richard and
Lynda Family Collection

Page 36-37: Lee Petty
Family Collection

Pages 38-39: Don Hunter

Pages 40-41: Lee Petty
Family Collection

Page 42: Top: Dorsey
Patrick; bottom: courtesy:
News & Record

Page 43: Top: Don Hunter;
bottom left: courtesy: News
& Record; bottom right:
Dorsey Patrick

Page 44: Top: Richard and
Lynda Family Collection;
bottom: Don Hunter

Page 45: Richard and Lynda
Family Collection

Page 46: Top: ISC Archives;
bottom: Don Hunter

Page 47: Tom Copeland;
sidebar: Bill Livingston

Page 48: Top: ISC Archives;
bottom: Don Hunter

Page 49: Kevin Kane

Page 50: Richard and Lynda
Family Collection

Page 51: Top: Richard and
Lynda Family Collection;
bottom: Kyle and Pattie
Family Collection

Pages 52-53: Kevin Kane

Pages 54-55: ISC Archives

Page 56: Courtesy:
News & Record

Page 57: Left: Kevin Kane;
right: Tom Copeland

Page 58: Top: News &
Record; bottom:
ISC Archives

Page 59: Top: ISC Archives;
bottom: Tom Copeland

Pages 60-61: Courtesy:
News & Record

Pages 62-63: Lee Petty
Family Collection

Page 64: Top: ISC Archives;
middle left: Dorsey Patrick;
middle right: ISC Archives;
bottom: ISC Archives

Page 65: Top: Kyle and
Pattie Family Collection;
middle left: ISC Archives;
middle right: Al Fortner; bottom: Tom Copeland

Page 66: ISC Archives

Page 67: Lee Petty
Family Collection

Page 68-69: Top left: ISC
Archives; middle left:
Richard & Lynda Family
Collection; bottom left:
Lee Petty Family Collection;
right: ISC Archives

Pages 70-71: Left: ISC
Archives; top right: T. Taylor
Warren; middle and bottom
right: ISC Archives

Pages 72-73: ISC Archives

Pages 74-75: Fletcher
Williams/Lee Petty
Family Collection

Pages 76-77: ISC Archives

Pages 78-79: Courtesy:
News & Record

Pages 80-81: Top: Daytona
Beach News Journal; bottom
left and right: ISC Archives

Pages 82-83: ISC Archives

Page 84: Kevin Kane; sidebar: Kyle and Pattie Family
Collection

Page 85: Top left: Kevin
Kane; top right: ISC
Archives; middle right:
David Chobat; bottom:
David Chobat

Pages 86-87: ISC Archives

Page 88: Richard and Lynda
Family Collection

Page 89: Top: ISC Archives;
bottom left: ISC Archives;
middle right: Tom Copeland;
bottom right: Tom Copeland

Pages 90-91: Kyle and
Pattie Family Collection

Page 92: Kyle and Pattie
Family Collection

Page 94: Kyle and Pattie Family Collection

Page 95: Top left: Hugh E. Carrigg/Kyle and Pattie Family Collection; top right: Kyle and Pattie Family Collection; middle right: Richard and Lynda Family Collection; bottom: Kyle and Pattie Family Collection; sidebar: Kyle and Pattie Family Collection

Pages 96-97: David Chobat

Page 98: Kyle and Pattie Family Collection

Page 99: David Chobat

Page 100: Kyle and Pattie Family Collection

Page 101: Top: Dorsey Patrick; bottom left: Kyle and Pattie Family Collection; bottom right: Kyle and Pattie Family Collection

Pages 102-103: Kyle and Pattie Family Collection

Pages 104-105: Tom Copeland

Page 106: Left: Richard and Lynda Family Collection; right: Kyle and Pattie Family Collection

Page 108: ISC Archives

Page 109: Kyle and Pattie Family Collection

Page 110: Top left: courtesy: News & Record; top right: Don Hunter; bottom: Don Hunter

Page 111: Tom Copeland

Pages 112-113: Kevin Kane

Page 114: Top: Tom Copeland; bottom: Bill Livingston

Page 115: Top: David Bundy, Montgomery Advertiser; bottom: Tom Copeland

Pages 116-117: Bill Livingston

Page 118: Left: Steven Patseavouras; right: Kyle and Pattie Family Collection

Pages 120-121: Mitchell Haddad

Page 122: Tom Copeland

Page 123: Top left: Tom Copeland; bottom left: Kevin Kane; right: Tom Copeland

Pages 124-125: Tom Copeland

Pages 126-127: Tom Copeland

Page 128: Tom Copeland

Page 129: Top: Bill Livingston; bottom: Tom Copeland; sidebar: Tom Copeland

Pages 130-131: Bill Livingston

Pages 132-133: Richard and Lynda Family Collection

Page 134: ISC Archives

Page 136-137: David Chobat

Page 138: Top: Kyle and Pattie Family Collection; bottom: Tom Copeland

Page 139: Brian Czobat

Page 140: Top: Tom Copeland; bottom: Jack Mellon

Page 141: Top: Kyle and Pattie Family Collection: bottom: Kevin Kane

Pages 142-143: Texas Motor Speedway

Page 144: Top: courtesy: Texas Motor Speedway; bottom left: Bill Livingston; bottom right: Tom Copeland

Page 145: Bill Livingston

Pages 146-147: Tom Copeland

Page 148: courtesy: News & Record, Nelson Kepley

Pages 150-151: Tom Copeland

Pages 152-153: Left: ISC Archives; top right: Richard and Lynda Family Collection; bottom right: Tom Copeland

Page 154: Top: Bill Livingston; bottom: Tom Copeland

Page 155: Tom Copeland

Pages 156-157: Tom Copeland

Pages 158-159: courtesy: News & Record

Page 160: ISC Archives

Page 161: Tom Copeland

Pages 162-163: Richard and Lynda Family Collection

Page 164: Top: T. Taylor Warren; bottom: ISC Archives

Page 165: Top: courtesy: News & Record; middle: Richard and Lynda Family Collection; bottom: Kyle and Pattie Family Collection

Pages 166-167: Bill Livingston

Page 168: courtesy: News & Record

Page 169: ISC Archives

Pages 170-171: Bill Livingston

Pages 172-173: Tom Copeland

Pages 174-175: Kevin Kane

Page 176: Left: Kevin Kane; right: Tom Copeland

Page 177: Left: Kyle and Pattie Family Collection; right: Kevin Kane

Pages 178-179: courtesy: News & Record

Page 180: Top: Kyle and Pattie Family Collection; bottom: Tom Copeland

Page 181: Tom Copeland; sidebar: Kevin Kane

Pages 182-183: Tom Copeland

Page 184: Kyle and Pattie Family Collection

Page 185: Top left and right: Bill Livingston; bottom: courtesy: News & Record; sidebar: Lee Petty Family Collection

Pages 186-187: Tom Copeland

Pages 188-189: Top left to right: Lee Petty Family Collection; Lee Petty Family Collection; ISC Archives; ISC Archives; Richard and Lynda Family Collection; Kyle and Pattie Family Collection; Kevin Kane

Bottom left to right: ISC Archives; ISC Archives; Richard and Lynda Family Collection; Kyle and Pattie Family Collection; Tom Copeland; Kyle and Pattie Family Collection

WHEN KYLE RETURNED to racing three weeks after Adam's death, Jeff Burton went over to Kyle and Pattie's motor home to give each a hug and express his condolences. Even now, what they told him remains with Burton.

Kyle said to never let a day go by where you don't tell your children that you love them and give them a hug. "Even if it embarrasses them, it doesn't matter," Burton says Kyle told him. "If you've got to grab them by the shoulder in front of all their friends and hug them and tell them you love them, just do it. I really think that's valuable. Through everyone's loss there's something to be gained. In most cases it doesn't outweigh the loss, by any means.

"That may be the best advice anyone could ever give. It's beyond advice about investments. It's beyond advice about how to be successful on a racetrack. It's beyond any advice I could imagine. Take your child and let them know that you love them. That's the core of what we are.

"When you bring someone into the world, you take care of them, you teach them, you cherish them, you let them know they're loved and, you know what, they do that too. It's what we do. It's what we ought to do."

It has changed Burton, the father of a daughter and son. "Adam's death and the conversation with the Pettys were a really sobering experience for me," Burton says. "It put some reality back into my life."